Building New Families

Through Adoption and Fostering

John Fitzgerald
and
Bill & Brenda Murcer

Basil Blackwell · Oxford

First published 1982
Basil Blackwell Publisher Limited
108 Cowley Road, Oxford 0X4 1JF, England

British Library Cataloguing in Publication Data
Fitzgerald, John
   Building new Families. — (The practice of social
   work; 10)
1.   Adoption
I.   Title   II. Murcer, Bill
III.   Murcer, Brenda   IV.   Series
362.7'34   HV875

ISBN 0-631-13148-5
ISBN 0-631-13193-0 Pbk

Typeset in 11 on 12 point Times by
Photosetting & Secretarial Services Limited, Yeovil
Printed in Great Britain by Billings, Worcester

Contents

Acknowledgements

Our thanks go: to Jane Rowe, OBE, who gave so much time to editing our written material, organizing it and reorganizing it, so that our three individual contributions could be married into one coherent manuscript. It was marvellous having someone like Jane available to us, who understood the essence of what we wished to convey about our work in this book.

To the Church of England Children's Society and in particular Miss C. W. Stone, who had the foresight to set up the Long-Stay Unit, supported us throughout our work at St Luke's and encouraged us to write this book.

To the staff of St Luke's, who gave so much of themselves to achieve the goals set for each individual child.

This book is dedicated to all the children with whom we worked in the St. Luke's Long-Stay Unit.

Editor's Preface

This book is about work with children whose family lives had been shattered. It describes how they were prepared for new lives in new families, introduced to their prospective parents, and given a fresh start.

It is thus of great relevance to residential and field social workers who deal with children. But its importance is far wider than this. Because it gives such detailed accounts of the effects of their family experiences on these children, and the efforts made to rebuild their security and confidence, it will be of real benefit to parents, step-parents, foster parents, doctors, teachers and many others who work with vulnerable children.

In our present society, many changes influence the experience of childhood. Higher rates of parental separation and divorce are only the most obvious factors. The widespread rise of unemployment and the deliberate running down of state support for families are other important elements. Research suggests that children in the age range five to 11 years are the most vulnerable to changes which threaten their security. If their parents separate, they are most likely to be deeply affected. If they come into public care, they are most likely to become isolated, losing links with their natural families, but not being helped to find substitute homes.

The majority of children described in this book fell within this age range, though some were a little younger. It therefore provides a valuable insight into the factors which make children of this age particularly at risk, and the ways in which they can be helped to master their fears and move forward confidently. These children had suffered a total breakdown in their family lives, but they provide important clues to parents and care givers on how to handle other less damaged children in their age group.

This is a book about specialized work with a small group of children with particular needs. It should therefore be read in parallel with other books about social work with children. In this series, we have already published Bob Holman's account of a preventive child care project on a council estate – a project sponsored by the same voluntary agency in which the St Luke's experiment was based. We have also published Tom O'Neill's account of residential care for mainly older children who were deprived of family life, and Nancy Hazel's book about the pioneering work in Kent to foster difficult adolescents.

In the introduction to this book, the authors put the St Luke's project in a context of child care policy. We should always be cautious about generalizing from particular social work experiments – however sensitive and skilled – into realms of wider policy. The children at St Luke's were some of the small minority of those who come into care who require permanent substitute families. The work was both arduous and rewarding, the outcome positive and encouraging. There are many similarities and many differences between this work and that going on in the new family centres for parents and their young children which many local authorities are establishing. Important experiments are also taking place in allowing foster parents to supplement the care given by natural families, rather than replace it, sometimes on a long-term basis.

Adults usually evade the distress which children feel when their emotional ties are broken or disrupted. This is one of the major reasons why so many non-custodial parents soon stop visiting their children, and why a high proportion of parents whose children remain in care for long periods lose contact with them. This book shows what can be done when adults have the courage to share these feelings with children, and to pay detailed attention to their reactions and needs. I very much hope that it will be widely read and used, wherever there are children in families that have broken, or are being 'reconstituted', as well as in the fields of adoption and fostering.

Bill Jordan

Introduction:
The Need for Permanence

This book has been written in order to describe the work we
undertook to help children who had suffered severe emotional
damage, in the hope that our experience may be of assistance to
others who are directly involved in work with children.
However, during the period that we worked at St Luke's in
Balham, South London, and in the time since, we have been
conscious of the rapid and varied changes that have occurred,
both in the overall organization of social services and within
those parts concerned with substitute family care.

The early 1970s saw the switch from local authority social
work specialization to genericism as the Seebohm Report was
implemented – something which was welcomed by some,
complained about by others. This trauma was followed by
another – local government reorganization – which left many
social workers with major structural problems to contend with
because of the break-up of some of the newly formed generic
departments and the formation of others.

In the wake of these organizational changes came a human
tragedy that was to impinge on the perceptions and practice of
social work at a variety of levels; the death of Maria Colwell.
The impact of the tragic death of this child was to change the
shape of an act passing through Parliament (the Children Act
1975), to bring about procedural changes that would affect
many child care cases, and to create a more cautious climate
within which social work was practised.

The death of Maria Colwell was partly responsible for a shift
of emphasis away from an all-embracing genericism in social
work departments to an increasing use of specialist skills, but

1

within generic settings. This change of emphasis was seen by many as reflecting the original intentions of the Seebohm recommendations.

During the period when local authority services were undergoing major change voluntary agencies, such as the Church of England Children's Society, had to struggle with a redefinition of their role, with the result that they have made a major contribution to the development of preventive and substitute family care services over the last decade. For example, whilst the Children's Society set up the Long-Stay Unit at St Luke's to help children move into permanent substitute families, it also set up exciting preventive work projects such as the one on a council estate in Bath whose report, written by Bob Holman, has been published in this series under the title *Kids at the Door*. In a sense these two developments epitomize what are all too often inappropriately perceived as conflicting social work interests.

Residential care has also undergone change during this period. At the beginning of the 1970s a large proportion of children lived in residential care following voluntary admission. Today, most will be subject to a court order of one sort or another, with residential care too often seen as a last resort. The debate around the appropriateness of using residential care for permanent care has caused confusion about its role. Some enterprising organizations, both statutory and voluntary, have developed family centres, where the residential provision is clearly temporary and the staff are involved in repairing damaged relationships in order to prevent family break-up. Others provide respite care for the medically handicapped and halfway houses for children leaving care at 18 to help them move towards independence. We are now moving towards a climate in which residential care will be seen not as an end in itself, but as a means to achieve specific goals for the benefit of children and their need for family life.

Substitute family care too has been changing in the 1970s. Fostering as a concept used to be fairly straightforward and could be described as 'short-term' or 'long-term' substitute care, whereas today the range of foster care available is wide, definitions ranging from short-stay through respite care, contract fostering, professional fostering, observation and assessment fostering and long-stay fostering, to 'fostering with a view to adoption'.

Adoption started the 1970s still very much as a means of dealing with healthy, illegitimate babies who could not live with their birth parents. Children in the care of local authorities, however, were rarely provided with adoption as an option, whereas today many more have this option available to them, despite the confusions that still remain as to whether adoptive or foster homes should be provided to meet their needs.

Two developments brought about this change. Firstly, a sharp decline in the number of healthy babies needing adoptive placements, as a result of many more single mothers keeping their babies and the wider availability of contraception and abortion. With fewer babies needing an adoptive placement, adoption agencies – both voluntary and local authority – were able to explore a wider use of their services. Secondly, the publication of the *Children Who Wait* study by Jane Rowe and Lydia Lambert[1] brought the real needs of children in care to the attention of social workers and their managers. This study identified the fact that once a young child had been in public care for six months or more he had only a one in four chance of returning home to his birth parents. This meant that for many of those children – the estimate at that time was 6,000 – life in public care, with its multiplicity of care givers and decision makers, was all they had to look forward to, unless permanent substitute family care with adoption as the aim was considered as an option.

It was therefore understandable that major efforts were made to find families for those children who had been in care, in many cases for several years. This resulted in the development of much more adventurous family-finding schemes, such as the use of television and newspapers to communicate the needs of waiting children. These experiments were followed by others, such as the establishment of adoption parties where prospective adopters and waiting children can meet in a social setting, or the wide-ranging use of photographs of children as a recruitment tool, culminating in a scheme called 'Be My Parent', a photolisting service. All of these developments were necessary and appropriate, but the attendant publicity tended to obscure, until the late seventies, the other significant conclusion of the *Children Who Wait* study quoted earlier, that once a child is received into public care, the first six months are crucial. In other words, if a child is to return home, there needs to be an intensive effort during this period to repair the links with home to enable him to return home as quickly as possible.

There is now a move in a few local authorities to ensure that clear early decisions about a child's future are made in order to provide him with permanence. The permanence concept was first developed in the United States in the mid-1970s out of a recognition that a child cannot have his emotional need for continuity of care met by a multiplicity of bureaucratic care givers, but only within the security of permanent adult relationships to be found in a family, whether it be his own family or a permanent substitute family.

Social policy in child care is shaped by a response to pressures from a variety of sources: the social work profession, the legal and medical professions, consumer groups on behalf of a range of people including birth and substitute parents, the media, political parties and society in general. Since the mid-1970s, permanence in the form of substitute family care has received a great deal of publicity, enabling those of us who have been involved to increase the opportunities of family life for those children who cannot return home. This has been appropriate and acceptable to society, politicians and the media. There has not been the same coverage given to the need for preventive or rehabilitative services, and this probably reflects the ambivalence and at times hostility, over this area of work, shown by some politicians and some sections of society. The danger, therefore, is for permanence to be seen as applicable to permanent substitute family care only and, in times of economic recession, to see it also as a cheap option. Neither is correct, nor is it appropriate to criticize the work that is being done in the area of substitute family care simply because society has not grasped the importance of preventive and rehabilitative services; they are all on the same continuum, each with its part to play.

Bill Jordan has expressed similar doubts about the polarization of view which sees preventive work versus permanence in terms of permanent substitute family care. It is not sufficient to see preventive services as short-term focused work, around admission into care, because such work could be carried out without any attempt at preventive work. Bill Jordan writes: 'The danger is that, in a climate of a shrinking role for the state, this model could be adopted without a commitment to prevention.'[2] Permanence should, therefore, be concerned with the repair to and maintenance of links between the child and his family of origin. He goes on to suggest that preventive work should be concerned with the idea of preventing children becoming isolated from their families of origin, rather than prevention of reception into care: 'the advantage of my definition of prevention, the prevention of isolation, is that it shows prevention and substitute care are inextricably linked, that one logically entails the other in any system of family and child care work.'

If permanence were to be construed in a narrow way, then the intentions of the founders of the movement would have been distorted. Jane Rowe has said that a concern only with adoption is 'the unacceptable face of permanence'. Permanence as a concept has a much wider context. It recognizes that permanence, if at all possible, should be achieved for a child within his family of birth. However, the focus of preventive social work with natural families should not simply be the prevention of reception into care. The aim of 'prevention' should be to preserve and strengthen meaningful links between children and their natural parents, and to prevent children becoming isolated through these links being broken or lost. Thus there are circumstances in which the appropriate use of residential care or fostering might be preventive, in the sense that it might be the best way of strengthening these links for the future.

The permanence movement also recognizes the need for clear planning, to enable social workers to provide the intensive support services to facilitate a return home, within a prescribed time span, of children received into care.

Only those children for whom major efforts to achieve rehabilitation have failed require permanence through adoption. The area of conflict comes over the setting of time limits in which to achieve rehabilitation. It is as inappropriate to pressurize a parent to give up a child for adoption when rehabilitation is a real possibility, as it is to pressurize parents to have a child returned to them when they are either unable or unwilling to be a parent to their child. Dr Christine Cooper, an eminent paediatrician, writes that 'divorce between spouses is now accepted; society should now accept that divorce between parent and child is sometimes needed. The parents should not be castigated for this.'[3]

Numerous studies have demonstrated how children have been allowed to drift in care because of a forlorn hope that one day they might be able to return home. In allowing the situation to drift, we fail to recognize that a child has a very different sense of time from that of an adult. For example, to a 30-year-old, three years is a relatively short time, whereas to a six-year-old it is half his life. These children can be left with a sense of alienation, are emotionally retarded and will often be unable to provide adequate parenting for their own children. Children who have grown up in care have some very harsh things to say about our inability to plan. Roy Parker quotes a girl's view after she had left care at 18:

> I thought they had all sorts of rotten plans about what should happen to me and I was bloody angry, because they wouldn't tell me. When I got older I realized that nobody actually had any plans at all. That hurt and made me more angry.[4]

The results of developing child care policies around a concept of permanence can be startling. For example, Betsy Cole, Deputy Director of the Child Welfare League of America, writes of the remarkable results achieved in two public agencies in the USA where this concept was adopted:

> In Michigan the switch of emphasis was responsible for 53 per cent of 305 children in care returning home within six months of reception into care. 81 per cent of the remaining children were either moving towards returning home or an adoptive placement.[5]

We can note that the emphasis is on rehabilitation, with adoption available only for those children who cannot return home:

In Maryland in 1975, the average stay in foster care was eight years. As a result of what is called permanency planning projection, in 1977 the average stay has been reduced to eight months.[6]

Nearer home, a handful of local authorities in this country have begun to implement a policy of permanence, and they too have found that they are able to return children in greater numbers, and more quickly, to their birth families. The Metropolitan District of Rochdale, for example, now claims to rehabilitate, within prescribed time scales, 85 per cent of children received into care.

Permanence in these terms means that most children in care can return home within a prescribed time span; however, it also means facing up to the fact that a smaller number will never return to their birth families. For this latter group, permanence should mean a placement with a permanent substitute family, and coping with the decisions about separation from natural parents that will follow as a consequence.

In our work at St Luke's the children we dealt with were in the main those for whom attempts at rehabilitation had failed, and where a placement with a permanent substitute family was the plan which could lead to adoption. The concept of permanence as we know it today had not been developed, but was implicit in our methods rather than explicit in our philosophy.

In writing about our experiences at St Luke's, we hope that we can demonstrate not only how residential and field social workers can combine to meet the need for skilled work with children, as applied to plans for permanent substitute family care, but also that the issues raised and the skills required apply equally to plans for children returning home to their birth parents. Their need for help to understand their past before moving into a plan for the future is just as great if they are to be successfully rehabilitated.

We also hope that we can demonstrate that children who have been buffeted by a number of potentially damaging experiences, both in and out of care, need sensitive preparation before an attempt is made to place them in permanent substitute families. The way we worked is not the only way, but all methods require the availability of skilled staff with time to devote to the task, and management support to enable them to make the most of the opportunity, if the children involved are not to face a further series of damaging disruptions. The danger for any area of social work practice in a time of economic recession is that resources for essential work will be cut and then, when problems arise, people blame the concept itself; the problems arising out of the implementation of the Children and Young Persons' Act 1969 are an example. Permanent substitute family care can and should be the objective of planning for children who cannot return home, but the service cannot be offered 'on a shoestring'. This form of care will be cheaper than public care in the long term, *but it is not cheap.* We hope that in describing our experience of working with children at St Luke's we can underline the importance of making available the resources of time, skills and finance to ensure that the children involved can look forward to a happy, secure family life.

1

How It All Started

The Long-Stay Unit at St Luke's, in Balham, South London, was born when the consultant psychiatrist said in an assessment conference: 'If you move Polly now I will not be prepared to accept the consequences.' His remarks confirmed the belief of the child care staff that this child should remain with us for further treatment rather than be subjected to what would be her fifth change of home at the age of three-and-a-half.

Polly's progress with us as our first really long-stay child was most satisfying to everyone concerned. After a period of treatment (described in chapter 5), she went to a new family and was subsequently adopted by them. It was as a direct result of our experience with Polly that others remained for similar help, though it was several years before we were able to achieve the staffing levels and methods of joint work between residential and field staff which were to become the feature of the Long-Stay Unit.

Until this time, children had spent only three to six weeks with us, as St Luke's was the reception and assessment centre of the Church of England Children's Society. Our facilities were available to the Society's residential establishments and fieldwork services throughout England and Wales, and were also used by some local authorities.

Up to 24 children could be accommodated, and the age range was initially five to 18 years. This of course excluded children in the Society's residential nurseries, some of whom were in need of special assessment. The age range was therefore lowered to two years, and after this there were usually some nursery age children in the group. Some children came direct from their own families, but there were a number who had experienced fostering and adoption breakdowns.

During the 1960s the Children's Society was the largest adoption society in the country and was placing up to 600 children each year for direct adoption or fostering with a view to adoption. Inevitably, in spite of much care, some foster and adoptive placements did not work out successfully and the children had to be removed. A period of assessment was often needed to allow appropriate plans to be made with care and insight. Other children referred to us were those who had spent too long in residential nurseries because some problem in their health, development or family had delayed placement in a substitute family, and there was still doubt about how best to plan for them. These youngsters had experienced trauma of a different kind but also needed much help if a happier future were to be achieved for them.

Work with the children in the assessment centre brought satisfactions and rewards which helped us to carry on against what at times seemed impossible odds, but during a child's short stay of three to four weeks we were very limited in the actual treatment which we could undertake. The most we could do was to find a way through to the child and pass on the knowledge we gained to the care givers to whom the child would return or, in the case of a breakdown in the previous care situation, to new ones. We did not agree with the people who said: 'You must find assessment work very frustrating and unrewarding as you cannot possibly hope to achieve anything within so short a time', because we believed that even brief relationships can be significant and may have a lasting effect. However, we came increasingly to feel that for some children a longer period of care and treatment was needed. One or two youngsters stayed a few extra weeks and evidently gained from this longer contact, but it was the decision to keep Polly with us which marked the real beginning of a treatment programme.

At first we simply had a few long-stay children in a small group alongside those who came and went following assessment. This pioneering stage enabled the Unit to prove its worth and taught us many valuable lessons. But various problems also arose. Resources which had seemed adequate – indeed superior to those available in most residential establishments at that time – proved insufficient. Out of sheer frustration, we got together as a staff team to define the aims of the Long-Stay

Unit in the light of the needs of the children being recommended for admission, and to look at the structure of the Unit in an attempt to identify the weaknesses which were impeding our work.

Experience had shown that there was indeed a need for therapeutic, individualized care and treatment for pre-school and primary school age children, most of whom had experienced a severe breakdown in family relationships and/or rejection by their parents or foster parents. For very few of them was there a realistic chance of returning home, but without special treatment another placement in a new family would be unlikely to succeed. We recognized that these children were becoming the focus of the work of the Long-Stay Unit and agreed that it would be appropriate to plan for the Unit to care for up to ten children under the age of 12 years.

Having come to this point, we could then see more clearly why we were experiencing stress and frustration over some aspects of our current work and staffing, and what needed to be done about it. We identified three particular areas of concern:

1 Staffing levels
2 Schooling
3 Relationships between residential and field workers.

Problems were arising because arrangements which had been suitable for reception and assessment work were not satisfactory for long-term treatment.

With hindsight it is possible to pinpoint some of the advantages and disadvantages of having the Long-Stay Unit attached to the assessment centre. All admissions to the Unit came via the assessment centre, and of course it was a major advantage that decisions about admission to the Unit were based on first-hand, extensive and intensive knowledge of each child.

It was also a great advantage that we already had a team with a variety of skills and with experience of a co-operative working relationship. The wardens, Brenda and Bill Murcer, were in charge of both the assessment centre and the Unit, and were intimately involved with the children as well as carrying administrative responsibilities. Residential and field staff, teacher, psychiatrist and psychologist were accustomed to pooling their expertise in a sustained effort to help each child. Every member of the team had a vital role to play and all recognized that none could function adequately without the others.

However, though specialist help was crucial and the established relationships eased the new developments, the overall conclusion must be that the Long-Stay Unit's attachment to an assessment centre was certainly not essential and was in some ways a disadvantage. The presence of short-stay children maintained our realism, but additional pressures were put upon staff by the complexity of working with two groups which had different aims and in situations which called for different degrees of involvement. The building which housed the Long-Stay Unit and the assessment centre was in many ways far from ideal for the task. Originally there were three separate buildings, built during the 1920s, that latterly had been linked at the back by a 60-foot corridor on the ground floor, and joined on the first floor to provide three separate units, one for boys, one for girls, and a wardens' flat.

The restrictions of the building limited the degree of separateness between the Unit and the assessment children to the provision of separate tables for children to share with their care staff, separate group bedrooms and a separate sitting room. There were two playrooms, but as their use tended to be determined by the type of activity which was taking place, their availability to both groups proved useful.

STAFFING LEVELS

When the Long-Stay Unit became firmly established, residential staff were allocated either to the Unit or to the assessment group. A ratio of eight residential staff to 24 children – which had been reasonably satisfactory for assessment purposes – was inadequate when long-term treatment was to be undertaken with some of them. Additional staff were therefore appointed so that there were four residential social workers for the eight to ten children in the Unit. (This was before the era of the 40-hour week. Our staff worked long hours and had only one day off each week.)

Work with the more disturbed children in the assessment group was a means of identifying those members of staff who had the ability, qualities and commitment needed for the work in the Long-Stay Unit, which was even more personally demanding. Most of the child care staff were young people in their 20s or early 30s, and few had previous residential experience. Many were students who came to us for a year or two as part of their preparation for future work or between courses. Some were studying theology or sociology but others had no obviously relevant educational backgrounds.

The ancillary staff consisted of a cook, domestic help, a laundress and a part-time secretary. Because it is obvious that household helpers are essential to a residential unit, it could be thought unnecessary to mention them. However, the ancillary staff were very much part of our team and as such were significant to the children, not only in the work which they did in the house, but as individuals who were part of the children's experience at St Luke's. Our West Indian cook was a particularly important person to our black children and was a great help in advising about their hair and skin care.

SCHOOLING

The children in the assessment centre went to the schoolroom for about three hours a day. The untrained but gifted lady who ran the class worked very effectively in conditions which had previously caused teachers to become discouraged and to leave. The emphasis was upon finding out what children had achieved scholastically, what their attitude was to school, in what areas they had problems, and the cause and effect of their difficulties. Although informal, the schoolroom regime was surprisingly effective in the case of the short-stay children. The findings of the educational psychologist confirmed this in the majority of cases. However, for the long-stay children of school age a trained teacher was needed with adequate facilities for continued education. A few of our children attended local schools, but the majority of these disturbed youngsters would not have been able to cope even if more places had been available. They needed remedial education, for which the overcrowded local schools had no facilities, and which could best be provided by a special unit within the centre. This had to be flexibly structured to meet individual intellectual, social and emotional needs. After considerable negotiation the Inner London Education Authority agreed to provide a teacher, equipment and teaching materials.

During the Unit's lifetime there were two teachers, both of whom were interested not only in education but in the whole child. They were sympathetic to individual problems and were prepared to be very flexible in phasing children into school attendance, setting up individual learning programmes and working with regard to social and emotional problems which affected children's performance. For instance, as Philip, aged six, sought to make sense of the emotional pain of his past and the confusions of his present, there were times when he could not cope with play in groups or school activity. When these occasions arose, the teachers readily recognized that his emotional needs were not compatible with his educational needs. They enabled him to withdraw appropriately from the group and then to re-enter in a day or two when he was ready.

The school-teachers saw themselves as part of the team and welcomed the services of the educational psychologist, who came each week to the assessment centre, and the guidance which his formal testing could give them. He could often offer advice and suggestions on activities which would facilitate or consolidate a child's learning. The teachers were present at reviews, submitted reports and contributed fully to the treatment plans and future plans for each child. The Unit's social worker was in constant touch with them.

SOCIAL WORKERS

As the treatment programme developed, it became more and more obvious that the Unit should not continue to rely on the social workers from the children's home areas to provide social work support and carry out the essential search for substitute families. Long distances were involved and the contact between residential staff, children and the various social workers who were attempting to find homes was minimal. This meant that it was not always easy for field social workers in the areas to appreciate the urgency of the need for prompt action. No one person was responsible for finding a new family for a particular child and so homes were just not available when needed. All too often we would reach a point in the treatment programme when the next phase should be an introduction to a new family, but none could be offered. Staff were beginning to despair and children to lose hope and to regress in their behaviour as the waiting time increased.

We felt that closer links between Unit and area fieldworkers would not only help to avoid these damaging delays but, by giving social workers more first-hand knowledge of the child, would guard against time being wasted by consideration of inappropriate prospective new families. It would also enable area staff to understand and, we hoped, appreciate our methods of preparation and introduction.

It was proving quite difficult to work co-operatively with some social workers and to achieve a sufficient degree of mutual confidence. We found that we were often not on the same wavelength in our communications during a planning session, nor in assessment of each phase of an introduction. Some fieldworkers had difficulty in appreciating or accepting our methods. They saw them as being overly fussy, and too demanding of everyone's time and effort. It was particularly difficult for them to appreciate the need to proceed at the child's pace. Some tried coercion, others had difficulty in resisting the coercion of their clients. Succumbing to pressures to take short cuts because of pressures of time, or over-eagerness for placement on the part of a child or new parents, had in hindsight been seen to be the cause of many past failures. We were beginning to be increasingly optimistic about our own methods, but felt that the chances of success would be enhanced if we could bridge the gap between the field and residential workers and field social workers and the child.

We felt this could best be achieved by having a fieldworker join our child care team. We needed our own social worker with time and commitment to recruit and select new families, someone who could also participate in the treatment and preparation of each child and facilitate introductions and the transfer to the new homes. We saw the role of the field social worker as being part of the link between the child's past, present and future. The emphasis was placed on flexibility, and when the worker was first appointed, some aspects of the role were deliberately left open for development according to individual skills and needs.

The children were encouraged to form their own view of this particular member of the team and to use what he had to offer in whatever way they chose. We felt that the new appointee's perception of the role had to be translated into human, non-clinical terms for the children with whom he would be working. Thus when Geoffrey, aged five, was found playing alone one day, he said he was playing social workers. Asked what social workers do, he replied: 'Play football and drink tea.'

Whether or not most social workers could identify themselves with this description, it should also be stressed that John Fitzgerald, the Unit's social worker, retained his position as a member of the fieldwork team undertaking the Society's work in South London. He was able to participate in the organized activities such as area team meetings, thus enabling him to retain a balanced view of the Society's work. Supervision was provided by the South London Area Social Work Officer.

The Society's Senior Manager of Residential Services was involved from the beginning of the Long-Stay Unit's life. Her participation facilitated its growth in a number of ways. These included the organization of forward planning, assisting staff to think through planning problems, relating the work of the Unit to the Society's overall policy, enabling staff to reach a satisfactory role definition and, as chairman of case conferences, bringing an objective and neutral influence to the decision making process.

In many ways, the Senior Manager was the individual who enabled the Unit to develop its own methods and identity, whilst at the same time retaining its place within the Society, thus ensuring that it did not develop in isolation. This proved particularly important as the work of placing children in substitute families increased. St Luke's work then had to be closely co-ordinated with the continued supervision and support which would be provided in the areas, since the Unit's staff could not offer long-term help to families living at a distance.

2

Our Philosophy and Approach

The basis of our philosophy at St Luke's was that the function of a residential establishment is rehabilitation. Care is not enough. We had one overriding purpose, and that was to restore children's capacity to live happily and develop healthily in a normal family setting. To achieve it we had to develop a treatment plan for each child. We found that an overall, generalized blueprint was quite useless – the individual strengths, problems and potentialities of each child had to be discovered and worked with in a coherent and planned way.

One of our earliest realizations was that deprivation is not a total state or experience and should not be used as a blanket explanation or excuse for a child's problems. We learned that areas of deprivation can be recognized and worked with in a courageous, positive way. We came to believe that both residential and fieldworkers can be too pessimistic about deprivation and shrug off difficult behaviour with an: 'Oh well, he's deprived, isn't he.' Courage is often needed by the adult as well as the child to face up to the pain, conflict or confusion which deprivation has engendered. But in reality few experiences are overwhelmingly bad, and even these are often encountered alongside at least some good ones. We sought to identify these good experiences and keep them alive by recognition and reinforcement through recall and symbolic repetition. We found that, provided the child was in touch with reality, much of the damage caused by past deprivation could be repaired. Children differ so much in their reaction to experiences and environment. Just as we all have to give up one stage to move on and reach the next, so with help a child can grow and gain from difficult and even depriving experiences which one would not have chosen for him in the first place.

We also believed in the expression of feelings and that feelings as well as facts need to be discussed. Genuine expression of feelings requires a free but supportive and accepting environment and the opportunity to build and test relationships over a period.

Given the right conditions, children can be helped to talk about their feelings concerning their parents and other issues of significance. An example is Vera, aged 12, who had been made the subject of a care order following problems at home. Her father had a recognized professional status and this seemed to impede the ability of social work staff to discuss with Vera her feelings about him. She was clearly unhappy, but communication with her was blocked. By acknowledging that it was Vera's feelings that were of importance, Brenda enabled this youngster to start talking about her past. Brenda acknowledged that the father was not an easy man to live with, and it was with great relief that Vera talked of the oppression to which she had been subjected. The key was to acknowledge Vera's right to express her real feelings about her father without fear of retribution from the other professionals now involved in her life.

The means we developed for putting these ideas into practice were a combination of a team approach and individualised care or 'specialing'.

'SPECIALING'

We recognized the importance of team-work and tried to practise it at all times, but we soon realized that, whilst every member of the team had something to offer, there was often one person to whom the child gravitated because of some individual aspect within the relationship which was being forged. This was often positive, but could be negative. It was through these special persons that the team worked by consultation and discussion. This system came to be known as 'specialing' and was an essential part of St Luke's methods. Among other benefits, it scaled down the demands of group living and protected children who had difficulty in getting on with people from the pressure of too many relationships when they were unready for this.

Since our task was to enable children to re-enter family life, it was essential that the pattern of care, social experience and relationships should be based upon and move towards a concept of normal family life. It was important to avoid a clinical atmosphere and to make sure that 'parenting' should be seen by the children to be the essence of the healing and educative process. Each house-mother's task was to care for the children according to their common and individual needs, giving more intimate care to one or usually at most two children who had accepted her as their special care figure.

Consistent mothering and continuity of care could not be fully achieved in the way it would be within a natural family. As in all residential establishments, the parenting task had to be shared, but every effort was made to maintain as high a degree of consistency and continuity as possible. The sharing of knowledge and experience of the child which went on constantly between members of staff ensured consistent handling and help in most situations which could arise. The special house-mothers provided day to day care, sat with 'their' children at meals, prepared them for bed and got them up in the mornings. They cared for 'their' children's clothes, took them shopping to buy new ones, took them to see the doctor or the dentist and shared as many of their personal and social experiences as possible.

We wanted the children for whom we were responsible to grow emotionally, but this involved risk for staff. To help each child, his special staff member had to give a great deal of herself and this meant developing an attachment. The child, however, had to move on, either back to his family or on to a new one and for his special house-mother this process was painful. We had to enable each staff member to let go, to mourn the loss of that special relationship. Similarly, the specialness of the relationship could lead to feelings of guilt when a staff member was off duty. To help them cope and to maintain continuity of care, we devised a method of nominating a substitute for a particular child for those occasions when his house-mother was not available. These arrangements were discussed fully with the child in advance and in so doing we hoped to avoid feelings of confusion in the child and guilt in the staff member concerned.

A TEAM APPROACH

In most social work settings the tasks of assessment, planning and treatment demand from each individual a variety of skills, an ability to perform a variety of roles and a capacity to contain or utilize anxiety, whether this comes from within the client or the social worker. These demands can be at their greatest in a residential child care setting in which the emphasis is on helping a child to cope with his own disturbed or conflicting inner feelings. We learned the importance of having available and making the best use of the wide range of individual skills from a variety of fields which could be found among the members of the team. This provided opportunities for shared experiences and supplied an added support system for staff and children.

Thus when Matthew, aged eight, was going through a particularly difficult stage, our consultant psychiatrist was able to help us all. Matthew had had a particularly painful past and had spent a year in a children's psychiatric unit. At one period he was liable to avoid going to the toilet until it was too late and would then spread faeces around the building. The impact upon staff was variable, ranging from confusion to outright anger. Our psychiatrist was able to help us understand that Matthew's behaviour was different, but perhaps normal for the emotional stage of development he was at – still only three years of age.

As we worked together to try to meet the children's needs, we found there were three prerequisites to a successful team approach. These were mutual respect, flexibility and communication. When any of these was lacking in an individual or situation we had problems.

Communication, especially communication with the children, was so central an issue in the philosophy and work at St Luke's that it will need a chapter to itself. The whole focus of our work was communication with and about the child. We had to share our knowledge of the child with the adults who were crucial to his future and, most important, we had to share it with the child – learning from him and reflecting back to him in a continuous and life-enhancing process.

The communication network spanned the child's past, present and future. In the past were parents, foster or adoptive parents, house-parents and social workers – sometimes all of these and more. All had valuable experience of the child and information about him to pass on to us. In the present were all the members of the team, not just those of us in everyday contact with the child but also the visiting consultants and the administrative staff at head office, whose interest and support were essential to the work of the Unit and the plans for each child. In the future were the natural or substitute parents with whom the child would be living when he left us. Most important of all was the child himself, the central point around which our communications revolved and with whom we had to find a way to communicate so that he could understand and come to terms with his past and present experiences and learn to master his future.

RESPECT AND CO-OPERATION

Readers from the social work world will, no doubt, have experienced situations where field social workers and residential social workers have been in a constant state of highly personalized conflict which places the individuals involved in a position where they need to take up a rigid stance in any discussion. Other common causes of conflict in residential settings are failure to appreciate the importance and value of the auxiliary staff's contribution or treating the psychiatrist as an outsider whose insights are feared and whose suggestions are ignored as impractical. The danger of splitting off one or more staff members from the rest of the group is ever present. We found it was essential that all members of the team understood each other's professional position, respected each other's views, knowledge, skills and integrity and offered each other full support. That is not to say that there was always one hundred per cent agreement – on the contrary! But, given the prevailing attitude of the team, we found that when disagreement occurred the matter could be talked through until the problem was resolved.

Mutual respect within a group or team is built in the first place on shared experiences. Once this climate is established, newcomers more easily take on the prevailing attitude, as they have the experience of being respected themselves and benefit from relationships with day to day colleagues and outside consultants. Few of the residential staff employed as houseparents had had formal social work training, so they had to learn on the job by example and much experience. Perhaps the quality most essential to their task was the capacity to demonstrate love by caring for the children, for any important figure in the child's past or future life and for other members of the team. This called for empathy, understanding, tolerance, warmth and compassion. They also needed emotional stability and maturity, with knowledge of any islands of immaturity in themselves which could impede their objectivity in helping children to work through fears, anxieties or areas of malfunctioning.

We sought staff with sensitivity to the need of others, people who were aware of their own limitations, willing to develop their own knowledge and skills, and ready to acknowledge and use the advice and skills of other members of the team. Acceptance and respect for individuals – adults and children alike – was also an essential part of a successful child care worker's make-up.

We were fortunate in being able to select our own staff, and we gave a great deal of time and thought to offering them appropriate understanding and practical help in dealing with difficult situations. We also had to demonstrate the arts of sharing and communication.

From the knowledge and experience which developed within a personalized 'specialing' relationship a house-mother could enable a child to reveal his personality and his problems. This intimate, first-hand knowledge of the child then had to be communicated to all members of the team, both for assessment and for the identification of areas where consolidation was necessary as part of the treatment plan. We found that this sharing of information was vitally important.

In spite of the value of individualized care, no one member of the team could have sufficient knowledge, experience, energy, time or skill to work exclusively with all aspects of any child's experiences and behaviour. To attempt to do so would have been unrealistic and detrimental to the child's future development. Each special care house-mother relied not only upon her own resources but also on the availability and support of colleagues and consultants to give advice, provide additional ideas and skills or to help her deal with the personal anxieties which were evoked by involvement with a child's problems and sharing his external and internal world. The work was emotionally demanding and team support was essential. At the same time, each member of staff had a real responsibility to ensure that communication within the group was ongoing and that each situation that arose, however trivial or painful it appeared to be, was discussed openly and honestly. Regular consultation sessions were held with each member of staff about his or her particular child. Each day occurrence sheets were completed on every child. It was part of the staff's responsibility to record both problems and the things that happened to the group, irrespective of how trivial the incidents seemed to be.

The importance of each incident, however small, being recorded and communicated to the rest of the group is illustrated by an incident involving a five-year-old girl, Valerie. During her early months at St Luke's, Valerie was unable to put her feelings of unhappiness into words. However, she told the special house-mother of another child that that child was unhappy. By ensuring that the statement, apparently concerning another child, was fed back to the rest of the group, a plan could be made that enabled Valerie to continue to use indirect communication about how she was feeling until she was ready to communicate directly with her own special house-mother.

The healthy staff group is the one in which an individual can challenge and be challenged. We wanted our staff to work together on problems from the inside out and ask how they could deal with them, instead of moving on and ignoring them. As a team we varied in age, life situation, experiences, interests, knowledge and skills. Collectively, however, we had a wealth of resources which could be tapped to give a variety of experiences upon which the children could draw.

The wardens, a married couple with two sons, had a flat within the main house and could provide a model of family life which could be used to the advantage of any of the children who needed special family-based activities, i.e. helping Mum and Dad with the housework, or odd jobs or seeing Mum and Dad washing, bathing, dressing, undressing or in bed.

The non-residential auxiliary staff were also all married people with homes and families. Their help was forthcoming for children who needed contact with normal family life. Children might need this to give them an awareness of family life, or as a context within which to recall anxieties which previous family experiences had evoked, or as a way of becoming familiar with what could at some stage become their new way of life. During these contacts the past could be recaptured and verbally recalled, or a future experience be discussed or anticipated. Some children needed such basic knowledge as seeing how a normal home is furnished or a family meal prepared. They had to learn how to appreciate and respect home comforts.

The single members of staff had their own special contribution to make in that they could talk about their lives at home, their friends, their boyfriends. They were able to take children home with them, or take them out with their boyfriends, thus often simulating a family outing with a mother and father figure. This not only widened the children's social experiences and showed them a variety of life-styles, but also enabled them to know that staff member in a fuller and more personal way. The social workers likewise brought family or spouse to visit the Unit and allowed the children to ask quite intimate questions about their home life.

Susan, aged four, would frequently say that 'mummies and daddies are bad'. Given her past experience this was hardly surprising. However, one way of redressing the balance was to let her see other happier families, so the Unit's secretary took her home to meet her mother and to meet friends and neighbours. Indeed, she became a regular visitor to that household and her view of mums and dads began to change. Recognition of the value of providing such opportunities, and the willingness with which they were made available, added to the climate of mutual understanding and respect within the staff team.

FLEXIBILITY AND CONTROLS

Flexibility was needed on several levels. We were all learning all the time from the children and from each other, so openness to new ideas was essential. We also had to develop new methods and this, too, meant willingness to try out different approaches and take risks with one's personal and professional self in coping with different situations.

Although we strove for flexibility in response to individual needs, ours was not a permissive establishment; in fact it tended to be rather protective, since this seemed best to meet the needs of the particular group of children we cared for in the assessment centre and the Long-Stay Unit. We saw organization, routines and procedures as a framework on which to build purposefully for our well-being. They gave order, predictability and a sense of security. As the majority of our children were tense, upset and often confused when they came to us, it was essential that there was a shape to the day that they could become quite familiar with and so relax enough to become integrated within the group as soon as possible.

The pattern of the day was structured with a balance of control, flexibility and freedom. There were times when activities were imposed, others when there was freedom of choice which allowed for self-actualization. The imposed activities were things like a few hours in the schoolroom during the morning; after lunch sitting quietly to read a book or watch TV or chat before going out for free play or for a walk or to play in the park; some quieter activity prior to bedtime such as reading, playing card games, board games or watching TV. The structure and pattern of the day helped disoriented or chaotic children, because the external predictable order could be internalized.

Expressions of negative feelings and manifestations of antisocial behaviour were a constant ingredient of life at St Luke's. Children needed to be allowed to ventilate negative as well as positive feelings. Staff needed to witness these episodes, because during or following violent emotional outbursts the child's deeper feelings, fears or anxieties were often frankly communicated and bonding took place. It was equally important that, if a child lost control and put himself or others in danger, a member of staff was at hand to exercise control and give comfort or reassurance when emotions had subsided. We were often able to help a child begin to regain control by saying: 'I know you are angry but I don't know why. Don't scream, say words, then perhaps I can help.' When all was quiet again we usually talked over the situation beginning with a question, not a censorious one such as 'Why did you behave like that?' but 'Why did you *need* to behave like that?' This set the climate for both child and member of staff to gain some insight into what was going on.

Naturally there were times when the lesson to be learned by the child was that what had caused the anger was the consequence of his own behaviour to another child, and the other child's or adult's point of view needed to be taken into consideration. If the child was sorry, an apology usually followed. However, the situation was not always that simple. Expressions of verbal or physical aggression sometimes occurred in a transference situation in which the child re-enacted past relationships and experiences. One of many examples of this was four-year-old Stephen, who was the odd one out in his family and was made the scapegoat whenever things went wrong. He was a mischievous boy for whom most things did seem to go wrong, because he went to excitable extremes which he lacked the ability to control. When others observed or intervened, he would defend himself by an uneasy, sometimes panic-stricken denial which often progressed to an act of aggression towards something or someone. It was quite a long time before he was able to become aware at a conscious level of the internal process of transference which was impeding his recognition of what was happening and his ability to cope in a different environment.

The need to be aware of the consequence of one's actions was the basis of our code of practice for discipline and sanctions. The code was drawn up in consultation with children and staff in a simple form of what we called 'Dos and Don'ts'. This set standards of behaviour and limits which should not be exceeded and gave positive guidance to safeguard physical safety and respect for feelings. Realistic and appropriate sanctions were exercised as necessary, taking into account each child as an individual. The fact that children were not necessarily all disciplined in the same way, and that a sanction was not always imposed, often brought forth the remark that is heard so much in children's homes and elsewhere, 'It's not *fair*.' It sometimes took a long while before the children fully understood that we treated them as individuals with differing needs and capacities. Any group of people living and working together needs a code to live by. What of ours? Some of it may sound idealistic, but it worked for us.

Our underlying attitude was 'we are in this together'. Together we can share the past which comes with us, share our present experience and look to the future. We can share our sadness, our happiness, and grow together towards a deeper understanding and a fruitful relationship. More particularly we believed that:

1 To serve the interests of the child is of paramount importance in child care. (This may sound obvious but it is difficult to achieve in practice.)

2 The best way of caring *for* a child is to care *about* the child. Do everything with love.

3 Be alive to the child and keep feelings alive within oneself and within the child.

4 Give respectful attention to each other and be completely honest.

5 Reach out to others to meet their needs, but in doing so encourage their self-respect. Encourage people to be themselves and allow them to make choices.

6 Help each child to face up to difficulties, and whenever possible to overcome them, by developing to his or her full potential of physical, intellectual, social and emotional strength.

7 Be optimistic and enthusiastic even when everything seems to be going badly. Keep faith and hope.

8 Accept what cannot be changed.

9 Endeavour to make a good relationship with each child

and adult within the group. Without it very little can be achieved.

10   To work together we must have fun together.

Putting all this into practice required constant and detailed attention to daily routines so that they could be adjusted and adapted to meet the current needs of the group or of individual children. The first of many plans was always how best to manage the admission procedures so as to minimize the distress and anxiety of what Olive Stevenson has called 'the cutting of the life-line'.[1] Coming into care or moving from one child care facility to another is always a frightening time for any child. We sought to establish right from the start a tone and climate which would demonstrate our care and concern for the children and our willingness to join them in their difficulties and to add our strength and support to their struggle for survival.

3

Communicating with Children

Many adults have problems in communicating with children, and social workers are no exception. An all too typical example of adult–child communication occurred one day at St Luke's when Peter, aged eight, met a visiting social worker in the corridor. 'Hello,' said the social worker quite abruptly: 'What's your name?' Back came the reply in just the same tone: 'Peter Smith. What's yours?' With this Peter ran off and so ended *that* communication.

Perhaps the first and major problem is that as professional people we often present only our professional self to our clients and are unwilling to share our personal, private self. We hide behind the professional mask and expect others to share their inner thoughts and feelings with us without receiving a similar response. This may work in a professional relationship with adults, but it does not work with young people. Children do not usually give themselves to an enigma, and so we must give them the chance to get to know us before they can trust us with their true feelings. Experience in the assessment centre and the Long-Stay Unit taught us that children will give us nothing until we have earned it and proved ourselves worthy of receiving it, and they can be quite ruthless in their testing and exploration. It is what we are prepared to give which will determine what we receive. We found that positive and constructive communication takes place only within a realistic relationship in which mutual understanding has grown from mutual knowledge. Through mutual interaction, two unfamiliar 'I's can grow into the 'we' who are relating to each other.

The building of knowledge of each other is vitally important in all social work with children. In a residential setting it can grow through shared experiences as well as verbal exchanges. While living together, children and adults come to know each other intimately, but fieldworkers also need to make a deliberate effort to spend sufficient time to be known.

Communication is a continuous process and occurs constantly at a variety of levels, both conscious and unconscious. We found that at all times our staff needed to be aware of what they were transmitting and receiving, because it was during shared experiences that the cues coming from the child were most easily picked up. Vitally revealing cues were there most of the time for us to work on if only we could recognize them. Not only was it important for members of staff to take every opportunity to learn about the child; they also needed to recognize situations in which the child needed to learn about them, to grasp such opportunities at the moment they arose, or even to create situations in which such learning could take place.

Listening, observing and empathizing have been described by Konopka[1] as the basis for good communication. To them can be added the creative use of all our senses – sight, sound, hearing and touch.

Effective listening takes time and the right attitude of mind. A number of teenagers who came through the assessment centre commented on the staff's willingness to take time to talk to them. They felt that lack of time to listen was a serious shortcoming of many of the busy residential workers they had known in the past, and they recalled times when information or support could have been of vital importance or resolved many fears, doubts and problems if only it had been made available. But time in itself is not sufficient. True communication also requires of the listener an acceptance of the other person and genuine interest in what he has to say. Within an atmosphere of true concern even painful questions can be asked and answered.

Observing is a way of listening to unspoken communication. Accurate, factual observations properly recorded are the first steps towards understanding, but the best observations also involve perception and intuition alongside common sense, intelligence and a framework of knowledge which enables the observer to make sense of what he sees. Thus a sound knowledge of normal child development is an essential beginning to useful observation of children with problems. Common sense may sometimes explain what appears at first sight to be an unusual phenomenon. So, when one of our new little girls seemed to have a peculiar gait, the house-mother quickly discovered that her shoes were two sizes too small, while another child, who was observed to be precociously self-assured over washing and dressing, was soon understood to be struggling to avoid the closeness of the small child's normal dependency on an adult.

Empathy, or the ability to put oneself into another's shoes, is probably the most essential element of fruitful communication. It enables the other person to feel safe and understood. Empathy grows with common or shared experiences and also depends a good deal on imagination and sensitivity. It can be practised and to some extent learned, though some people seem to be innately good at it.

Since play is the way in which all children learn to cope with the environment, it is a natural and most effective method of communication. It is difficult to enter the world of any child, let alone a deprived and distressed one whose experience of life may already have been more traumatic than anything the helping adult has yet had to face himself, but shared play can provide a way into a child's world.

Mary was such a child. At three years old, she was much too independent and self-contained. She was emotionally flat and lacking in response to any attempts to encourage emotional interaction of any kind. She depended on no one adult and refused to get close to any of us. We knew that she had not lived with her mother but had visited her from time to time. Their relationship was a shallow one in which the child's experience had been of a casual and repeatedly rejecting adult. We found that Mary frequently wanted to move from table to table for meals, contacting different adults each time. We wondered if this were a symbolic continuation of her having inconsistent mother figures with whom to relate in real life. She used to awake screaming during the night but gave no indication of why she was upset. It was so difficult for us to enter Mary's world and share it. Brenda eventually found a way to communicate with Mary, which she subsequently wrote up in the following report:

I went into the schoolroom one morning with a group of young children. Mary sat down at the table wanting to draw. I got her a paper and a pencil. She then said: 'You draw like me.' I joined her and we sat together drawing. Mary drew a dog then a few people, saying: 'That's a man and that's a lady.' To one of the other children she said: 'Draw a Daddy like me – I draw a Daddy.' I asked: 'Do we like Daddies?' Mary: 'Yes, you draw a big Daddy like me – look, he's got some eyes and a nose.'

She then said: 'You do a house', but went on to draw one herself. I asked: 'Who lives in your house?', to which Mary replied: 'Mummy. She makes a cup of tea. She says hello Mary and I come to her and I come back.' I asked: 'Are you going to Mummy again one day?' Mary: 'I'm coming back here to stay – right?'

After a while she told me what I was to draw next. 'You draw a ghost, I'm drawing a ghost.' I asked: 'Where does the ghost live?' Mary replied: 'In his dark. You draw on my paper.' One of the boys came in at this point and shot me with a toy gun. I remarked: 'Are you shooting me?' Putting her arm around me, Mary said: 'I keep you. Don't shoot her, she's my friend.' When the school-teacher arrived I got up to leave the room and Mary came too. As I picked her up and carried her to the kitchen, I noticed that for the first time she was moulding to my body. From entering into Mary's world in this play situation I had at last reached her feelings. For a brief time we were close, but shortly after this episode she moved away from my table and resisted continued closeness. However, I now knew what she was afraid of at night, even though she hadn't been able to verbalize her fear.

In another play situation, playing at a little girl helping a Mummy with her work, we reversed roles after a little while. I became Mary and she Mummy. After helping Mummy for a while I said: 'I tired, I lie down.' I shortly awoke crying out: 'Mummy I frightened. Why am I frightened?' She rushed to me, put her arm around me saying: 'It's de ghost.' I recalled that the ghost lived 'in his dark', so we switched on the light and sent the dark away so that the ghost couldn't live in it. Later in the garden and on many ensuing days Mary came over to me and spontaneously stalked and killed 'my ghost'. She ceased to wake screaming in the night.

One's first meeting with a child is a very delicate occasion when more than the normal defences are likely to be erected. What must be conveyed immediately is respect for the child as a person and all channels of communication need to be brought into play to receive cues from the child and transmit messages back on an appropriate wavelength.

At St Luke's our first meeting, when the 'case' became a child, was often on the doorstep. Visual observations gave the first cue from the child's posture, his facial expression and his physical position in relation to the escort. We learned a lot initially from the interaction between them. We also found that if we gave our attention to the escort in preference to the child we missed the initial opportunity to transmit the message that the child is the most important person.

A welcoming smile and a warmly welcoming tone of voice were our first offerings, followed by social give and take. If we were not introduced, we learned to say who we were and why we were there, i.e. 'I'm Mr Murcer. I live here.' One might go on with: 'Have you come a long way? Did you come by car, train or bus? What did you see on the way?' Thus we communicated in neutral zones before getting down to the important realities.

The vital question to be asked of every child irrespective of age was: 'Why have you come here?' We learned that this seemingly difficult question could be asked in just these words provided the tone of voice communicated the message 'I would like to know because I am interested and I want to understand.' But before this central issue is tackled, one needs to sense the child's inevitable anxieties and convey to him the message that his mixed and painful feelings are accepted – indeed expected – since everyone in a new environment feels insecure to some degree. With most children it helps to put this into words since, even if they cannot explain their feelings verbally, it is reassuring to hear the adult express and accept the unhappiness and confusion.

Whereas a normal family may be able to get by with a minimum of overt communication, treating deprived and traumatized children requires a constant effort to communicate. We really tried to communicate all the time and to teach the children to do the same. Poor verbal communication was initially a problem common to most of them. As well as providing opportunities for them to express themselves through play, we tried to teach them to use words as well.

We gave all the children as much opportunity as possible to hear adult conversation as well as talking between adults and children. We always spoke to children in passing, we spoke to them in play. We sang together and made up songs about each other or about what we were doing. During bathing, dressing and undressing we sang 'This is the way we wash our arms, face, neck' etc., we counted buttons and stairs. When laying tables we talked about who sat where, and similarly with all other domestic tasks we used words as well as gestures to explain what we were doing and why.,

Singing games and action songs were always popular and family games such as tea parties, putting dolls to bed or pretend outings gave opportunity to introduce another range of words and to hold imaginary conversations. On real outings we tried to be alive to everything that was going on around us and to help the children be the same by commenting on what was going on and trying to see things through a child's eyes.

Another useful medium for communication was playing 'Conferences'. The children were curious about what went on in the weekly case conferences and we were able to put this interest to good use in a game which could be adapted to varying needs. John Fitzgerald was the subject of one conference during which the children explored interesting aspects of his childhood and parents, his wife, his work etc. In short, they were getting to know all about their social worker as a person.

On other occasion, when the children chose to confer about 'My Mummy', one of the little girls told us many things about her mother. Although we already knew some of the facts, it was valuable to hear them from Annie herself and learn her feelings about them. In this play setting she was able for the first time to speak critically of her mother's behaviour. This confirmed our belief that Annie was coming to terms with her past. It helped us to consider the kind of parents she needed and influenced our choice of a new family for her. The game also provided opportunities for us to tell children facts about themselves which they needed to know.

One of our central themes at St Luke's was – whatever happens, consult the child, communicate with him on all levels whenever you have the opportunity. To staff we used to say: 'Never hesitate to admit your ignorance to children. If you don't know – ask.' Learning follows listening and whatever kind of response one gets is a communication which gives a cue as to what must come next. A rebuff or even negativism has a message. We found that the children themselves are a most reliable source of information about what has gone wrong in their past. They are reacting to their individual interpretation of the facts and circumstances of their lives. One can do no better than learn to read them as they learn to read books, by looking, learning, listening and relating their behaviour to their past experience. However, it is important to check the facts, for the child's interpretation may be quite different from the reality.

Equally important is communication through caring. The provision of comfort, good physical care, control and the opportunity to have fun is the residential social worker's first and best medium for communicating acceptance and concern. Whether we like it or not, the activities involved in daily living together are all a form of communication. The way a child's hair is brushed, or meals are served or games are organized all convey important messages about how we feel about children in general or this child in particular. These activities provide a constant background of communication. There are also many opportunities for therapeutic non-verbal communication in response to a child's unspoken need. Philip provides a clear example.

In his own home, Philip had often been left alone in his room in situations when he really needed help either of a practical or emotional nature. One day in his early weeks at Balham he had a tantrum at the meal table when he could not allow himself to accept help with cutting his meat. Any attempt to pick him up from where he had flung himself to the floor increased his rage. He eventually quietened as he rocked himself despairingly to and fro. When he had spent his anger the house-mother simply said: 'You must be very tired, come and sit on my lap and I will rock you.' His relief and satisfaction were apparent as he fell asleep. We decided that it might help Philip if rocking could become a happy, comforting experience in the future. Seated on the lap of an adult in a rocking chair and listening to some favourite songs was one of the ways in which he learned that adults could be good people to whom he could trust himself, who could provide pleasant experiences to balance the pain. This was his first experience of our sharing of pain and pleasure and of our practice of giving support during re-creation of a frightening experience. We were communicating by touch, sound and hearing, and the rocking proved one of our most effective tools in helping this deeply deprived and bewildered child.

4

Treatment

The children referred to St Luke's were generally manifesting their problems in ways which were detrimental to their own well-being and the well-being of others. Most of them had suffered rejection by their families and came to us bearing the scars of their emotional wounds. Some of them had suffered actual physical neglect or personal and social deprivation, others had lacked stimulation and opportunities for normal maturation and healthy relationships. We learned by experience that most of our children were too damaged to grow out of their difficulties without specific help. Treatment of their emotional problems was essential to future progress.

The areas of retardation and the stages at which development had been arrested varied according to their previous experiences. In addition to rejection, the presenting problems could have been caused by a variety of factors, for example: distorting mothering, over-indulgence or repressive control, inappropriate demands for cleanliness or bowel and bladder control during toilet training, or pressure for performance beyond the child's capability in physical, intellectual, emotional and social spheres. Excessive moralization, abnormal identification or the influence of subcultural social codes were other potential causes of the child's distorted development.

The resultant behaviour problems which would have to be treated could include bed wetting, soiling, inhibited or repressed aggression, over-aggressiveness, tantrums, destructiveness, lack of feeling and consideration for others, defensive lying or blaming of others, and taking their possessions. Sometimes lack of verbal stimulation had caused a poor level of verbal expression or communication which in turn could cause either inappropriate acting out of feelings or impaired thinking and reasoning ability.

As participant observers in a variety of daily activities, our first task in the Long-Stay Unit was to identify the areas in which the child needed special help. A start had always been made on this during the child's stay in the assessment centre, where admission procedures were seen as a crucial part of assessment and treatment. They are described here in detail as an example of the ways in which we tried to work. We learned that very careful planning around admission was an essential preliminary to treatment.

Before deciding that admission for assessment was appropriate, we had of course received considerable written information from the child's area social worker and sometimes had the benefit of face to face discussions and conferences. If the social worker involved was already familiar with St Luke's and could help to prepare the child and his family well in advance this was a great benefit, but in any case the date and time of admission were planned with the social worker so that arrangements could be discussed in detail. We always stressed that consideration of the child was of paramount importance. We aimed at arrivals well before a meal time and early enough in the day to allow the child to settle in before bed time. We asked that children should bring their own clothes no matter what their condition, and toys from home, particularly a comfort toy or object. Their things from home would serve as reassuring objects to which they could hold on in the loneliness which comes in the midst of an unfamiliar crowd. We hoped that whenever possible parents would come along too, so that the child could be secure in the knowledge that his parents knew where he was and thus feel less abandoned and lost.

Work also had to be done to prepare the staff and the other children. Relevant information passed to staff always included the child's name and age, a brief account of his background, his relationship to the escorts, the expected time of arrival and who would require meals. There were often personal circumstances that it was vital staff should be aware of so as to avoid unnecessary stress during the early introductory period or to ensure that what should be a particularly happy time was not overlooked. Two extreme examples will illustrate this point.

Albert came to us after he and his father had spent a homeless night on a railway station. The day of his arrival was his birthday. Although it was only a matter of a few hours since we had been asked to take him, Albert and his father sat down to a birthday tea complete with candles and presents.

A terrible tragedy brought Mary and Michael to St Luke's at equally short notice. Their father had murdered their mother in the next bedroom during the previous night and they had witnessed the arrest of their father only a few hours before they came to us. Staff needed to be aware of what had occurred and to protect the children from unthinking questions about why they had come to us.

When they saw preparations being made for others to join them, the children needed at least to have their curiosity satisfied. If they were interested beyond that point, they usually asked questions. Their attitude depended upon whether they saw the new child as a possible friend or a possible rival. No matter what the reaction, we encouraged them to have a caring concern and mentioned ways in which we could all give help.

Practical preparations began before the day of arrival whenever possible so that there was no danger of the child feeling unwelcome by finding no place prepared for him in the house. A bed was made up, flannel, towels, toothbrush and hairbrush were provided in the bathroom and marked with his name. A safe place for his treasured possessions was made ready. Prior to his first meal with us, a place was laid in the dining room for the child and his escorts. We saw these preparations as a reinforcement of the welcome received on arrival.

A door opened wide by a member of staff who pleasantly greeted the child and escorts was the first introduction to St Luke's. They were then shown into a homely sitting room just inside the front door in which initial social exchanges and a cup of tea could reflect normal family hospitality. Fears and anxieties about the unfamiliar place and the unfamiliar people within it heightened sensitivity and emotions at such times. It was important that everyone should be put at ease in a personalized setting and that the member of staff should present a personal self as well as using professional expertise and knowledge to deal competently with the situation.

A verbal picture of the centre was given, including the composition of the group of children and staff and an outline of the pattern of the day and the activities within it. Discussion of the child's personal functioning usually followed, covering areas of health, diet, sleep, interests, leisure time pursuits, likes, dislikes – in fact anything to give us sufficient understanding to meet the child's needs rather than frustrate them.

This sharing of knowledge revealed not only facts but the attitudes and feelings which surrounded these facts. It gave us an insight into attitudes, feelings and behaviours which were a reaction to the past environment as distinct from those which were a response to the new, present environment, and helped us to understand how the child's past and present might interact to affect or determine the immediate and long-term future.

The escorts and child were then shown around the house and came into contact with other members of the household. Always there were more pleasant greetings which were an extension of the first welcome. During this initial contact the child had the continued support of familiar figures and the escorts were gaining a shared knowledge with their child which could be mutually supportive after separation had taken place. This would safeguard against a possible unrealistic anxiety being transmitted which could be destructive of the peace of mind of either of them.

For some, physical separation was to be temporary, for others it would become permanent. Whatever the plan at this stage, before the escorts left and in the presence of the child, the anticipated length of stay was discussed and arrangements were made for future contacts. These might be in the form of telephone calls, letters or visits. For some the purpose of contact was to keep in touch until restoration could take place; for others it was to be a process of disengagement with the past.

Although parting can be a sad and painful experience, we ensured that it was a conscious event for the child and that the member of staff involved in the reception of the child was present to keep control of the situation and give appropriate help for as long as was necessary for the child to come to terms with it. Other members of staff became involved only when the child was ready for this and at a time or in circumstances which would not heighten anxiety or distress.

From the moment each child first came to us, the careful record of relevant events, observations, attitudes and feelings increased the sensitivity and understanding of the residential staff. The record also provided additional information for the consultants, i.e. the doctor, educational psychologist and psychiatrist, all of whom would see the child later in a clinical setting.

Working within our overall philosophy, we endeavoured to enter into the child's world, to play an appropriate adult role, to gain empathy and understanding. We listened and watched for direct and indirect clues and cues which indicated the areas in which we ought to provide help. We tried to give this at the most opportune time which, more often than not, proved to be immediately the need was manifested.

In planning a programme of treatment, we had to identify which behaviour was caused by a child's sickness and which by immaturity of development having regard to age and the stimulation or lack of it within the child's previous environment. We also had to take account of effective intelligence in relation in innate intelligence and we learned never to underestimate a child's intellectual capacity, irrespective of the findings during the initial psychological testing. The IQ of some of our children increased dramatically during their stay with us. Tom was said to be educationally subnormal before admission to St Luke's. Our psychologist tested him and got the same result at first but later, when he had won Tom's confidence by playing football with him, he prepared a further series of psychological tests and found he had an IQ of 140.

The treatment plan for each child had to encompass as many aspects of life as possible. Staff needed to set up a comprehensive programme of experiences and to share in those experiences either directly through participation or indirectly through discussion. The child's 'special person' always took a key role but received a lot of support from senior staff. Quite often, less experienced people needed help to see that methods which would normally be acceptable might be inappropriate in the treatment of a particular child. For instance, putting a troublesome youngster out of the group might be a reasonable way of achieving control, but for a rejected or depressed child it would reinforce feelings of unworthiness. Often house-parents needed specific suggestions about how to deal with problems like stealing or constant defiance.

Sometimes we needed to provide experiences which a child had missed to enable him to go forward from a more secure base – for example, an opportunity to correct past mistakes or misunderstandings. Before this could be successfully accomplished we had to study the child's pattern of behaviour and listen to what he had to tell us. A lot of the children's less acceptable and antisocial behaviour was defensive. It was for us to learn by discussion and observation what they were defending against. It was for us to learn from the children themselves and not make assumptions from the facts as relayed or recorded by others. We learned by experience that children react to their own interpretations of facts and these are not necessarily the facts as adults understand them. We came to realize that they often misinterpret things and need help to appreciate the reality of circumstances or situations.

Although for some separation from their previous families held an element of relief, they were often very confused about what had gone wrong. Barry had been rejected ever since his single mother had married a much older man who did not want a child, but Barry felt that his mother had ceased to love him because he wet his bed. At first he thought that if he could be dry he would be able to go home.

We learned gradually, and sometimes unwillingly, that the painful experiences of the past could not be left to sink into the unconscious to fester and cause later problems, but must be brought out into the open and dealt with by sharing them and offering support. At first, like most adults, we were reluctant to do this, fearing to add to the child's distress and seeking to protect our own feelings. With the help of our psychiatrist we gradually realized that it was no kindness to leave the child alone with his problems and our belief that things should be shared committed us to share pain and through sharing give reassurance and comfort.

A fairly obvious example was the case of Janet, who came to us from a private foster home where she had gone after the death of her mother. Mother had died in hospital and the child had been protected from participating in the realities of the situation. For Janet, her mother's death was an abstract event.

When we talked with her about it she said: 'Mummy went away into hospital and she died. When she comes back I shan't go to see her.' Because Janet was the youngest member of the family, her father had thought it would be better for her to be fostered, and so she was deprived of the opportunity to mourn with her family. Instead she reacted against what she saw as rejection by her mother by difficult and aggressive behaviour with other adults. This led to the breakdown of the private foster home and Janet's referral to St Luke's. When our psychiatrist recommended that the finality of death must be discussed with her, we felt as if we were killing her mother, yet it had to be faced up to with the child. She needed to talk about it a number of times, going over the facts again and again until she could accept that her mother really was not coming back.

Janet also had to understand that she would not be going back to her family. This was done in a positive way, emphasizing her father's belief that at her tender years, Janet needed the mothering which he himself could not give, and reassuring her that as she was a little girl without a mummy to love her, we would do our best to find a mummy who needed a little girl to love. She accepted this but expressed concern about her father. 'Who will look after him and get his meals?' She was just four years old. Young as she was, Janet had been told the truth in a way which she could understand, by a person with whom she had made a bond in the early part of her stay and thus she could come to terms with reality and move forward to a new life and a new home without guilt or conflict of loyalties.

This case also illustrates another important point about dealing with painful realities from the past. We found that before we could do this safely and effectively we had to have a good base on which to build. A child cannot deal with pain constructively until he has had some positive experiences and reassuring, safe relationships. If we had tried to deal with the problem of Janet's orphan status when she first came to St Luke's, she would not have been able to cope and would have rejected the idea and us too.

The use of the word 'treatment' tends to conjure up a clinical setting, but this we strove to avoid. We wanted to provide an environment that was as normal as possible, relaxed but richly satisfying, emotionally undemanding and yet not entirely stress free because this would be unrealistic and our children had to realize that other people have needs too, and learn how to give as well as take.

The psychiatrist was a very familiar figure to the children as well as the staff at St Luke's. He saw them for assessment and follow-up sessions. As the Long-Stay Unit developed, he took on some children for therapeutic sessions. For most, however, treatment was through their daily care and activities. An abundant supply of the ordinary nurturing offered in any good family was the most appropriate way of treating many of the problems presented. Often this could be provided in very down-to-earth ways.

For sublimation of aggression, messy play can be not only therapeutic but fun. Provision exists in every home for water play in the bath and in the washing-up sink. Dirty potatoes can be scrubbed and dirty floors mopped clean. The garden yields puddles and mud. A sand-pit can give an opportunity for messy play in the construction and destruction of sand pies and castles. Toys and tools for banging, such as drums, hammers, wood and nails offer outlets for anger and tension as well as being aids to imaginative and inventive play. The release of repressed aggression can be helped by encouragement towards teasing relationships – kindly ones of course – romping and friendly fights with other children and adults. Role playing can also provide symbolic and verbal release of aggression.

For the child who has been under too much pressure to achieve, the opportunity for success and praise for small achievements can help to balance success with failure and provide the incentive to accept, to come to terms with and, if possible, to overcome problems and limitations.

Some children actually had to be taught how to play, even at the simplest level of rolling a ball back and forth. We encouraged staff members to join games, helping children to sustain their imaginary roles of milkman or bus conductor or helping to keep the peace by themselves taking the role of policeman. It was important that senior staff show by example that playing with the children was a serious part of their responsibility, brought no loss of dignity and was not considered 'slacking'.

Everyday life in a residential setting provides many

opportunities to help children learn suitable self-control as well as how to express feelings. We often used simple contracts such as: 'If you are quick in the bath I will read you a story.' 'If you will help to set the table, you can choose what you would like for lunch.' In this very basic way, children learned something about reciprocal relationships.

A number of the children who came to us had previously lived with adults who were disturbed in some way, and they needed good models with whom they could identify. Sometimes we had to demonstrate and teach socially acceptable ways of relating to others. As no one can claim to be perfect, we found that recognition, explanations and sometimes an apology could help a child toward a realistic acceptance of other people's shortcomings. When Pauline ran into the road her house-mother was so frightened that she slapped her hard. Later she apologized and explained how scared she had been. When Robert broke a window with his ball while he was playing with Brenda Murcer, she went with him to apologize to Bill Murcer and spoke for both herself and Robert, saying they felt scared about what they had done. This made a big impression on Robert, who often recalled the incident and remembered every detail of what was said. In these little ways we could offer a child hope of achieving a good enough pattern or standard of behaviour to be social acceptable and efficient. Counteracting other negative influences could be tackled in the same way.

Quite often, we needed to help a child catch up on basic knowledge. One of Jim's problems was difficulty in learning colours. We reinforced his attempt to learn by having red, blue, green and yellow days. Jim would wear a jumper which was the colour of the day, lay his table with crockery which he selected from the crockery shelves in the colour of the day, and at afternoon sweet time would pick out Smarties which were the appropriate colour. As he was allowed to eat the ones he identified correctly, he succeeded in learning his colours.

Percy provides an example of seizing an opportunity to give specific treatment, when it arose in a natural way. When living at home Percy had been locked in his room for hours, sometimes days at a time. The educational psychologist had reported: 'Percy uses a pencil well. It would be useful for him to be shown how to draw a house, etc., so that he begins to notice details presented on paper, in preparation for schooling. He maintains verbal contact when drawing and is ready to absorb considerable information about the world about him.' Yet when we tried to encourage Percy to draw a house we found that emotionally he was not yet ready to do so. His damaging experiences in his previous homes were still very evident in his personality and behaviour. The following account of how Percy came to terms with his feeling about houses was written at the time:

Percy walks boldly into the office, quite relaxed, smile on face and twinkling eyes: 'Can I play with you for a bit?' Phone rings, so before answering it I say: 'While I talk on the phone, would you like to play with this Lego set?' P.: 'Who you talk to?' With hand over phone I say: 'It's Mr L. and I shall be a long time.'

P. opens box and looks at the pictures on instruction book, places book back in box carefully and pulls a chair up to office desk. Jumps up nimbly and kneels on chair, and with thumb and forefinger carefully selects a base and begins to build. P. becomes very absorbed in his building, phone call ends but I still hang on to phone. Without looking up he says: 'Why you not talking?' 'I'm listening, P.' 'Oh', and continues his building. He now has six rows of bricks in an oblong shape about six inches by three inches. Without saying a word I reach into the Lego box and carefully select a door and hand it to P., who looks at it, turns it over and over, finally returning it to the box. He continues to build upward until he has eight rows of bricks. Since I handed him the door, he has fidgeted quite a bit yet still appears absorbed. Now, licking his lips frequently, he scratches his face, wipes his right hand across his mouth and generally looks a little ill at ease.

P. now begins to pick up roof tiles, has some difficulty in fixing them together and says: 'Come on, you help.' I replace the phone without a word and he begins to hand me roof tiles. When the roof is almost completed, quite out of the blue he says: 'You didn't say goodbye.' 'No, P., I didn't say goodbye.' He reaches over and takes the roof from me and carefully places it on top of his house. 'Finished.' 'How do you get into your house, P.?' He places the house under his arm and quickly walks out of the office, avoiding my stare. I follow him out of the office and up the stairs: he places the box-like house carefully in his locker, shuts the door and chases off to the playroom.

Percy was not yet ready to create a home of his own. Was he afraid that unless he put up barriers he might in his fantasy – which at his age was not yet divorced from reality – find himself back inside his other own home, where he had suffered rejecting social and emotional damage?

Several months later, Percy again walks boldly into the office, saying: 'I want to build a big, big house so that people can live in it with me.' He begins to build and puts in the first window. I ask: 'Does your house have windows?' He ignores the question but looks at me as if I were stupid, of course it is to have windows and doors. The building has two floors, so it is expanding and becoming more accommodating. He talks anxiously about the fact that it might burn down, leaving him with nowhere to live. We talk about what would happen if St Luke's caught fire. He then said: 'I want a big house just like this one.' He was confirming what we had already observed.

Children like Percy often have difficulty in expressing their fears verbally, sometimes because of an impoverished vocabulary, sometimes because they are heavily defended against relating positively to an adult or trusting themselves to adults. In seeking to help Percy prepare for school, we had achieved the even more important goal of learning more about what was troubling him and helping him overcome his anxieties.

In Sheila's case we quite deliberately set up a situation in which we could help her by sharing in what had been a traumatic, anxiety-laden situation.

Some of the demands made upon Sheila by a rigid and perfectionist mother had been beyond the child's physical and emotional capabilities and inevitably led to emotional stress in her relationship with adults. She was expected to be socially responsive, have impeccable table manners and her toilet training had been forced. Sheila was very small for her age and had difficulty in sitting on an adult sized toilet. Left alone to cope in her previous setting, she inevitably wet her knickers, sometimes because she was afraid of falling into the pan or because of the physical effort involved. She had come to us with the reputation of being a dirty child, at the meal table, in her play and particularly in her apparent disregard of toilet training. We decided that she would always be accompanied to the toilet by a member of staff. Sheila was told that this was so that she could be lifted on to it because she was not tall enough to climb on. The reason was also to help her to overcome her tendency to avoid dependency upon us. Going to the toilet was one of the very few situations in which this child could permit herself to accept help. It was also a time when she would talk to us.

One day when Brenda accompanied her to the bathroom, Sheila said: 'I don't like you because you smack little girls when they are naughty.' Brenda assured her that she did no such thing. As they sat there together Brenda asked her: 'Why did you come here, Sheila?' She answered: 'I told my mummy to pack my case and she did and I came here.' Having been reassured that this adult didn't smack little girls, the next question was: 'What will you do if I wet my knickers?' Brenda told her that she would give her a dry pair and wash the wet ones. A few days later Sheila tested this out and learned that Brenda could be trusted and could understand her difficulties.

Occasionally something more dramatic was needed. Gloria, at 14, was older than most of the children in the Long-Stay Unit, but she came to us in urgent need of help when the children's home she was living in refused to keep her any longer. Undoubtedly Gloria was difficult. Sometimes nothing pleased her; she contradicted and wilfully misunderstood everything and everybody.

One day, when everyone was at their wits' end, John Fitzgerald and the teacher offered Gloria a game of tennis (she loved tennis and was very good at it). We then turned the tables on her by deliberately miscalling balls so that what was out was called in and vice versa. Gloria was first confused, then furious. After a time, John explained that they were reflecting her own behaviour to other people. Gloria took the point and the game resumed in the normal way. She often referred to this tennis 'lesson' and some years later successfully tried the same method on some girls who were being difficult at work.

Another unconventional treatment occasion was set up to give children a vivid demonstration of how their unruly behaviour affected others. Several of them had been behaving very badly, roughly pushing others off the chairs in the schoolroom and causing much noise and disturbance. The staff group agreed that something must be done. The children were sent to watch their favourite TV programme and then the adults who had identified which child they intended role playing, rushed in and began behaving as the children had previously done. The youngsters watched wide-eyed and rather scared. When the staff ended the performance and asked the children what they thought was happening, one of the little boys said: 'You're out of control.'

Treatment plans were made and revised and progress was monitored at the regular conferences held on each child. Progress was often uneven, and it could be encouraging to find that whereas a child seemed to have stood still in one area of development, he had perhaps made gains in another. We tried to be realistic as well as optimistic and did not expect to do more than make a good beginning at treatment during the child's stay with us. We knew that some things from the past could be dealt with only during the process of placing the child in a new family or back with his own parents. Some problems would take years to work through and we could only make a start and build a bridge from the past and into a *specific* future. One cannot treat a child in a vacuum, and we worked with a plan for a permanent placement always in mind.

5

Polly, Anthony and George

POLLY

Background information

At two months old Polly was admitted to the Society's care and placed in a residential nursery. Her single mother had requested that she be placed for adoption. At this period very large numbers of babies were being offered for adoption and suitable homes were not always immediately available, especially if the infant had even minor health problems. Polly's placement was delayed.

During her early months in the nursery she was described as a frail, pale baby with mild infantile eczema. But though this worried her at times, at 10 months old she was considered a normal, happy and responsive child. A year later nursery reports describe Polly as making slow progress, easily upset, not very happy and wary of new people. During this period, the nurse who had special care of her had left and a new young nurse took over.

As Polly became attached to her new 'nursery mother' her progress improved, as did the eczema, and it was decided to board her out with a view to adoption. However, at the same time the nursery was closing and in the weeks immediately preceding her fostering placement Polly had the alarming experience of seeing all the other children leave. Her nursery mother and most of the other staff also departed.

The nursery staff had felt the prospective foster parents were suitable and Polly apparently liked them, but unfortunately the placement was not a success. Polly had sleeping and eating problems and was negativistic. Within two weeks the foster mother said she could not cope and had not taken to the child, so Polly was placed in a children's home. Here, too, her behaviour gave cause for concern and the house-parents considered her a very disturbed child whom they could not understand. She was admitted to St Luke's Assessment Centre for psychiatric advice. It was Dr Crosse's strong recommendation that Polly remain at the Centre which started the whole development of the Long-Stay Unit.

House report for case conference (two months after admission)

Physical appearance and habits
Polly is aged three years one month. She has grey/green eyes, thin straight blonde hair and a square-shaped pale face. Appears to have a slight squint in her left eye and there is evidence of eczema on knee flexors but it is not active. She appears to be physically normal for her age, is capable of dressing herself and can do up her buttons.

Polly has only a moderate appetite and was initially very difficult with her food. She would regurgitate food if pressed to eat against her will. She is toilet trained, dry by day but very occasionally wet by night. Sometimes wakes for toilet during the night. On three occasions during the first week of her stay, she awoke screaming, trembling and perspiring. Responded to comforting and settled in bed sucking her thumb under the cover of a hanky

Her speech is variable. She consistently says 'No/hello/bye-bye' distinctly, is capable of echoing speech correctly and on occasions spontaneously says short sentences distinctly. Most of the time, however she babbles incoherently.

Out of doors she plays on swings, tricycles and the pedal car. She will push other children around in the car for long periods. Indoors she likes rocking toys. Watches programmes for young children on TV but loses interest from time to time.

Behaviour and personality
Polly was escorted to the centre by Mr and Mrs B., house-parents. She appeared to be shy but smiled when spoken to. For a time she leaned defensively against Mrs B.'s knees. Her first day at the centre was the quietest and least eventful. By tea time she was more bold and was talking a little. Enjoyed her bath and settled happily to sleep through the night.

On her second day the battle commenced. She had by this time attached to her house-mother, was following her around and wanting to be carried. She occupied herself by imitating her rather than playing with other children. She looked very unhappy, whined if overlooked by her, yet resisted attention from anyone else with a violent 'no' followed by screaming and aggression. She would, however, relate superficially from the security of her house-mother's arms.

Polly manifests the behaviour of a depressed and withdrawn child and is tyrannical in her own defence. Help or persuasion with meals bring on tantrums which leave her exhausted. Unwelcome attention distresses her and brings forth verbal and physical aggression. However, even during her worst periods, we see glimpses of her brighter side through her response to humour and improving responsiveness to some members of staff.

She is capable of responding warmly to affection and occasionally gives it spontaneously, but is inclined to follow it up at times with aggression. She is obviously genuinely upset by change in environment and nurture but appears to be able to accept help, judging by her improvement so far. It will be interesting to see if her speech will improve as she matures. Taken in isolation it would appear that speech therapy should be considered.

Attitude to adults
For a time, Polly reacted violently to being handled by anyone other than her regular house-mother. She next accepted the plumper lady members of staff and has finally begun to relate to other male and female members of staff. She is at varying stages in her relationship with each individual, but spontaneous affection is reserved for her first contact house-mother. Polly tends still to be rather unpredictable in that she is quite likely to kick or scratch when approached, according to her mood. She tends to seek attention by being aggressive rather than affectionate. She understands what is said to her but is at a loss to communicate verbally because of our failure to understand her gibberish speech.

Attitude to other children
Following the pattern of her behaviour with adults, she first chose one child – a boy a little younger than herself – for more favourable attention. She was very aggressive with the younger children and very upset by retaliation. She sought refuge by sitting next to an older boy in an effort to avoid relating to anyone, yet resented his taking an interest in her. She is now fond of all the older boys and treats them in much the same way as the adults at the centre. She had gone out of her way to be affectionate to new little children on the day of their arrival, after which time they have become victims of her ambivalent attitude and targets for her bat, in preference to a ball. She prefers not to be

part of a group and, if she cannot wander off and find individual attention, she will overwhelm the adult whose attention she requires by aggressive behaviour towards him or her as well as to rival members of the group.

Psychologist's report for case conference

Test results

Merill-Palmer Scale

Chronological age	37 months
Mental age	31
Percentile rank	12

Behaviour

Polly was negativistic and hostile and firmly rejected any personal approach. Seated on a familiar adult's knee she co-operated better than on her own, but either way she showed adequate concentration and persistence with some of the tasks while flatly refusing others.

Assessment

The test results show inferior abilities, but their reliability is questionable because of Polly's negativism and because of the rather wide scatter of scores. Failures and successes extend from the 18–23 months range as far as the 42–7 months range.

Language development is clearly retarded, although the extent of the retardation is uncertain because of the child's doubtful co-operation. She was able to copy single words rather indistinctly, but not groups of words. Spontaneous intelligible speech was limited to 'hello' and 'no'. Her comprehension of speech, however, seems better developed and she was able to understand simple instructions.

Polly showed considerable variation in performance skills. She could not fit a number of blocks into a box (18–23 months level), nor in spite of determined efforts could she cut with scissors (24–9 months), but she buttoned a four-button strip nimbly and quickly (42–7 months).

It is concluded that Polly is not a mentally defective child. Her negativism undoubtedly affected her performance of the tests and, although she is retarded in speech, in other aspects of development she is probably nearer average than her test score suggests. A more adequate assessment could be obtained when she is nearer school age.

Psychiatric report
When I first saw her, Polly refused to leave the group and no attempt was made to compel her to do so. She was negativistic but this trait seemed superficial, as she made a half-hearted attempt to relate to me.

A few weeks later I found her very negativistic. She cannot generalize her relationships, e.g. will relate fairly easily to plump people only. Any attempt to remove her from the group again caused distress and she quickly appealed for emotional support and had to be carried about.

Her speech is unintelligible but she can say a few words clearly. Gives the impression of being morose but this is poorly maintained, as she smiles and has a sense of humour.

Rather strong-willed and perceptive in a social sense. Rather violent likes and dislikes.

Opinion
Difficult to give an opinion yet, as she requires time to verbalize her feelings and ideas. Signs of a serious mental disturbance. She is not yet fit to be moved from Balham.

Treatment plans
The decision of the conference was that Polly should remain at the centre for therapeutic help in the Long-Stay Unit. The initial treatment plan was as follows:

1   An extended stay to give more stability.
2   Individual personalized care, with opportunities to make a more positive relationship with her special care figure and then to generalize her relationships.
3   Attention to be given to stimulating and developing her speech to enable her to verbalize her feelings and ideas.
4   Review in three months' time.

In Polly's case, as indeed in all the others, we found it very instructive to spend time considering her past experiences. As usual, this exercise shed a lot of light on her present behaviour and guided our efforts to help her. This child's aggression and her fear of change were easy to understand in the light of her obvious need to cling to every shred of security she could find. She had experienced loss of her closest care takers, she had seen her first known environment disintegrate before her eyes, had suffered rejection by foster parents and then had to adjust to a children's home in the middle of a busy town with a totally different environment and regime to the nursery in the country which she had previously known. The different noises and smells, the size of the children, house-parents rather than uniformed nurses – no wonder she had sleeping and eating problems and was tyrannical and self-defensive.

Fortunately, the St Luke's house-mother to whom she immediately attached herself was positive, firm, compassionate and consistent in all her dealings with children. At this time we had not yet developed the system of a 'special person' for each child, but we knew from her history that Polly had progressed well in the nursery until her special nurse left, and her current need for immediate and consistent availability of a trusted adult was so great and so obvious that we saw a special relationship as essential to her recovery, and set about rearranging systems to make this personal care possible.

The benefit to Polly lay in being able to scale down her interaction with adults to a level she could cope with, and the benefit to the rest of us was that the special house-mother could build up a deep understanding and rapport with this disturbed little girl. Through observation and through discussion with this house-mother, the rest of us learned how to handle Polly so that consistency of approach could be achieved and confusion and conflict minimized.

Whenever possible Polly's special house-mother not only undertook her personal care but sat with her at meals, and was either with her when she was playing or allowed the child to come with her while she undertook other work. If she was not able to be available she would explain why this was so. Much depended on the co-operation of other staff members in being willing to take over other jobs if Polly had a genuine need for her own house-mother to be with her.

The rest of the staff tried to relate to Polly in neutral and indirect ways and in non-threatening situations by smiling or laughing when she was being amusing and by relating to other children with whom she was playing. Even this indirect approach could stir Polly's aggression and hostility, but she had to learn to tolerate it. As we attempted to get closer to her while she was being 'protected' by her special person, we accepted her hostility without retaliation. In this way she was able to externalize and work through her anger, finding that it was safe to do so.

Gradually it became possible for the rest of us to offer Polly symbolic tokens of affection so that she could learn again that she was lovable and could love again in return. When kissing other children, we would say something like: 'I know you'll probably smack me, but I want to kiss you because I think you're gorgeous!' Without this sort of approach Polly would have lacked help in letting down her defences and tolerating affectionate advances from adults. Until she could do this she could not move into a family setting. Although it was sometimes painful learning, it was an essential step to achieving the basic underlay of security in love that would enable her to go on to accept the firmness and even anger of others. Polly had to discover by experience that what she was learning from her special person could be applied to others who could also 'love the doer but hate the deed'.

Although she understood more words than she could say, Polly's vocabulary was limited. She could not tolerate many people talking directly to her, but she needed to be among people talking in all sorts of situations and in all sorts of moods. As well as exposing her to as much adult to adult, adult to child and child to child conversation as possible, we took every opportunity to talk to Polly about everything that was going on and particularly about any special interests she had, such as dancing.

As we tried to enlarge her vocabulary and her tolerance of people, we gradually widened Polly's horizons beyond the Centre and into the community outside. We took her on the bus, to the shops, to the common and to visit members of staff in their homes. These new experiences were not always easy. Some painfully re-created earlier situations, but by going through them with adults who recognized and understood her feelings she was able to emerge a happier and more secure child. After a subsequent interview with Polly the psychiatrist was able to report:

A substantial improvement in the emotional state when compared with her assessment on admission ... She has recovered from what appears to have been a severe depression. Her relationships have improved beyond all expectation.

Polly moved into a family after a year at St Luke's. She settled well and was much loved. Adoption followed six months later.

ANTHONY

Early history

Anthony was originally admitted to the Society's care on a temporary basis, as his young single mother hoped to make a home for him. However, six months later she asked that he be placed for adoption. She was getting married and her future husband would not accept another man's baby.

After three months in a short-stay foster home, he was placed in a residential nursery. Here he made good progress, milestones average. He fed and slept well and was a happy baby with a pleasant disposition. He did periodically bang his head against the cot before going to sleep, but this had stopped before his placement in a foster home at the age of 18 months. In this home, Anthony initially made progress, but after a move to London, the foster family experienced financial difficulties and this caused tension in the home which naturally affected Anthony. The Society's social worker was concerned about the child. He was not given enough mental stimulation and his physical state also deteriorated. It was decided that, in spite of the risks in breaking the emotional ties which he would have made to this family, it would be in this little boy's best interests to be removed from the foster home. He came to the Long-Stay Unit via the assessment centre.

House report for conference (Three months after admission)

Anthony is aged three years and seven months. He has light brown hair, blue eyes and a square-shaped face. On admission he was very pale and undersized, had a distended abdomen and very thin legs and arms, the muscles of which were very flabby. He walked around in a sluggish, lethargic manner, like the old man that his face gave the impression he was. He was a compulsive eater and concentrated on his food to the exclusion of everything else around him. This continued for some weeks but is now less noticeable. He slept well from the first and seemed not to change his position during the night. At this time he was occasionally enuretic at night but very rarely by day.

In recent weeks Anthony has had a lot of flatulence and diarrhoea and the doctor finds that he is anaemic, but we have observed a gain in weight and he is nearly up to average for his age. His limbs are fatter and his muscle tone has improved. He has also become more agile and active.

Behaviour and personality

Anthony was escorted to the centre by his foster mother and Mrs C., his social worker. Foster mother introduced Brenda Murcer as the Aunty who was going to have him for a holiday and teach him to hop, skip and jump. Anthony resigned himself to listening to foster mother 'going on' and responded mechanically to her instructions. He parted from her without distress.

For some days he was over-controlled emotionally, resistant in areas where he had obviously been pressurized at home, lacking in initiative, spontaneity and in a sense of fun. He took everything literally and if we tried to suggest different interpretations he would say: 'Don't you contradict me.' He could not play with anything but a toy car and took about a week to relax and become more spontaneous. He began at this time to play in a simple social sense and began to accept affection. When asked at this stage if Mummy cuddled him on her lap he replied: 'When Mrs C. comes.'

Interests

Initially he played in a depressed mechanical manner with a toy car. He has no idea how to play with dough and was unhappy when he got his fingers dirty when introduced to finger painting. At first he ignored other children and then, when he did try to play co-operatively, he clashed because of his tendency to commandeer the play material.

Attitude to adults

In spite of the fact that Anthony performed tricks for us when he first came, in other respects he was resistant to attempts to make a personal/special relationship. He was demanding of help and tried desperately to control us. He gave the impression that he was automatically trying to resist being repressed by us. His remarks were obviously echoes of adult remarks at home, so he seemed very much to be like a little old man in conversation too. He was just too serious for a toddler.

He began to make relationships through simple social play and has recently begun to expand this into the emotional sphere. Staff were highly delighted to hear him cry and seek consolation one day last week when he hurt himself.

Attitude to family
Foster father and foster sister visited on one occasion. Anthony was pleased to see them but did not get emotionally involved. After having pushed Anthony for a short time on the swing, father soon transferred his attention to a group of boys playing football in the garden. Foster mother has rung three times but has not visited. Anthony's remarks about his foster parents reveal the lack of social and emotional stimulation in this home.

Summary of problems
1 A child who has been over-controlled and given orders to the point that he now lacks spontaneity and waits passively to be told what to do.
2 Unable to use his imagination.
3 No idea how to play.
4 Too much attention has been paid to his lack of agility, so he is self-conscious about trying.
5 He is too flabby and fat and lacks muscle tone and normal three-year-old 'bounce'.

Treatment plans
It was decided that the best way to help Tony with a number of his problems would be to concentrate on helping him to play more freely and creatively. This would not only improve agility and muscle tone, but more importantly would be a basis for helping him to relate to adults and children, and would, we hoped, enable him to begin to express his fears and fantasies. It would be through play that a child of this age would largely come to terms with the loss of the family he knew, since verbal discussion would inevitably be limited.

At first it was necessary to go back to the very beginning of social play and show this little boy how to play like a baby and interact with someone by rolling a ball back and forth and similar very simple games. From this, he gradually progressed to more imaginative games of tea-parties, playing bus conductor or garage attendant. Staff members needed to be actively involved in many of these activities to enable children such as Anthony to sustain a role and learn how to develop ideas. A wide variety of simple toys and materials were made available to him at all times.

It was important in this child's case to try to avoid giving him instructions and to get him to think for himself. Learning to choose was not only vital for everyday life and making decisions, it would also be crucial for Tony – and others like him – to understand and then break away from his past and involve himself positively in decisions about a new family.

This was a child who needed to learn to express anger in appropriate ways and channel aggression into acceptable activities, otherwise when his hostility was released it would get him into a lot of trouble. He had to be introduced to rough and tumble games with adults and children and learn to cope with mild teasing.

Progress with Tony was quite slow overall, with spurts and set-backs. After a year at St Luke's, when the staff were beginning to think of a new family for him, he showed that he was not yet ready for this by going berserk on a visit to a staff member's home. It was the first time he had been with an ordinary family since his admission and it was clearly too much for him. However, six months later, after a lot more work and some very positive experiences, his ability to relate to people was much improved. His IQ score, which was 95 on arrival, was now 122. Though his imagination was still somewhat constricted, his play was notably richer and more spontaneous and he was an altogether less passive person. A nice liveliness was indeed emerging and a capacity to test out and make demands was sometimes a little too much to the fore! Bill Murcer summed him up in a conference report as: 'A lovable rascal. He will give foster parents a good deal of stick but the rewards of fostering this child will easily outweigh the inevitable difficulties.'

It was agreed that Anthony was ready for a new family, but that the family would need special qualities, as he was likely to test the strength of the relationship, would probably be very demanding and possibly rejecting and negative. His placement is described in later chapters.

GEORGE

Background information

George was born of a short-lived and stormy marriage. His father was from Pakistan, his mother white. George was only a few months old when his parents separated and he had no further contact with his father. For the next three years George was cared for by his maternal grandmother, who was very fond of him. His mother formed a liaison with another man and had two babies in quick succession. Her emotional health had always been fragile and she now became subject to depression. Her feelings for George were always very mixed.

Problems really started when the grandmother died very suddenly. George was alone in the house with her and they were not found for some hours. His mother took him to live with her. At first things went quite well and there was even talk of George being adopted by his stepfather. But then the stepfather discovered that George was half Pakistani – his mixed racial descent was not noticeable in his colouring – and he thereupon completely rejected the boy. George responded with difficult and disturbed behaviour and became incontinent day and night. His mother applied for him to be admitted to the care of the local children's department, but before anything could be arranged she found a private foster home and placed him there.

Here again things went well at first but then deteriorated, and the foster mother often threatened to give up. Then, when George was five-and-a-half and had just started school, his mother suddenly decided to take him home again. Once again, after a few months, problems became acute. George reverted to wetting and soiling day and night. He would stand in front of his stepfather and urinate. Twice he was found with matches trying to start a fire. He also refused to eat, became increasingly withdrawn and would not play with the younger children. Outside the home he appeared a normal child, but as soon as he returned it was as if a curtain came down over him. To add to an already complicated situation his mother became pregnant with twins. She was increasingly agitated about George and her husband still rejected him. He was admitted to care and placed in a short-stay foster home.

Shortly after this his mother had a miscarriage, and blamed the loss of the twins on George's upsetting behaviour. She said she did not want him back and asked that he be placed for adoption. At this point George was admitted to St Luke's for assessment and treatment

Excerpts from reports for first conference

House report
George is a small, attractive six-year-old boy with brown hair, dark brown eyes and an oval-shaped face. He is capable for his age and tried to be very independent at first. He now accepts adult help.

Bedtimes are difficult for him and he has trouble getting off to sleep. In spite of this and early waking, he appears to have sufficient sleep – at least there are no obvious signs that he is tired. There is nothing in his file about toilet training, but it must have created problems for him. He waits until he is at bursting point and then jumps up and down frantically clutching at himself. If we suggest he goes to the loo before going out for a walk he becomes resentful and denies he needs to go, yet almost before we turn the corner he starts his war dance.

When first admitted to Balham, George was far too accepting of the situation. He was anxious to select his bed and put his clothes away, saying with great feeling: 'I like living with lots of children.' Actually he is very much a loner and rarely mixes with the group. He has many aches and pains but, though he exaggerates them, he cannot accept physical comforting from an adult.

Only rarely do we see brief glimpses of a happy, carefree boy, as most of the time he looks troubled. He is very fragile with both children and adults and is easily crushed. At first he was unable to talk about his background at all and when the subject of mummies and daddies came up he would opt out. If asked a direct question he immediately changes the subject, but he has begun to make occasional references to home.

Psychologist's report
George is of above average intelligence, IQ 116, but is retarded in reading skills. This seems somewhat surprising as he has a healthy test profile, sound vocabulary and normal hand/eye control.

Psychiatric report
George is an attractive, good-looking boy of above average

intelligence. He seems to have a very engaging personality and made an immediate good relationship with me. He played happily and quite constructively, talking in a sensible and intelligent way throughout.

During the conversation he made a few remarks about his second house and his third house. He did not volunteer any information about the death of his grandmother, and blocked when I put some more direct questions. He told me that his mother had told his father to beat him even though he had not done anything wrong. He blocked on any information or feelings about leaving them and blocked almost completely on his recent stay with foster parents.

His play became more boisterous and he sought a lot of physical contact, which he clearly enjoyed. I then realized that there was a seductive element in this, culminating in his telling me that he had a pain in his groin. This, coupled with his fearless, flirtatious approach to a total stranger, makes one wonder about a number of things and possible incidents in his past. This ready attachment must be to some extent pathological and there is evidence of very considerable denial and dissociation. Rather surprisingly, he let the interview session be terminated without any protest or clinging or attention-seeking behaviour.

In all, George presents a picture of a rather institutionalized child, in spite of the fact that he has not spent any time in institutions. I do not think any of the problems are irreversible, but suggest the need to seek a permanent placement as soon as is consistent with good child care practice.

Treatment plans

As with Polly and Anthony, George's problems stemmed very obviously from the deprivations and traumas he had endured, and knowing a good deal about his past made it easier to plan a treatment programme for him.

He was clearly defending himself against anxiety by being over-controlled, which meant that he could not let himself go to sleep and could neither accept help nor confide in adults. We recognized that there was little hope that he could come to terms with his past until he could relate to us on a personal and social level. He needed to be the loner and lost in the crowd until he was confident that people would not be punitive and rejecting.

The plan was to let George take his own time, to reach out to him in play and in neutral areas of daily life. To force the pace would be to strengthen his defences and make him feel even more vulnerable. We recognized that he might need to regress while he mourned the losses of his past, but there was encouragement in that he appeared to have had a good relationship with his grandmother, which would provide something positive to build on.

It was agreed that he should be gently encouraged to form an attachment to a house-mother with whom he could let down his defences and begin to talk about his family and their treatment of him. While this was going on, careful observation, good teamwork and detailed reporting to each other would be essential. We also recognized that George would probably have to reject his mother and stepfather before he would be able to take on a new family. On a practical level, he needed individual help with reading so as to ensure that his good potential was not overlooked.

The first step forward was an improvement in his ability to trust adults. At first, when anyone indicated that they understood how he felt or tried to comfort him, he was very tense. His hand, when held, remained as unmoving as a block of wood and he was very sensitive to any type of correction, no matter how mild. The breakthrough came one evening when George and some boys were shouting in the bathroom. Eventually the house-mother asked George to leave the bathroom and not come back till he could talk in a normal voice. He went out, but was found shortly afterwards standing in a corner looking very pale and frightened. The house-mother suggested that if he wanted to cry it was all right to do so, and she knelt down and held him in her arms. He burst into violent sobs and said: 'At the other house I was forbidden to cry.' After this it was easier for him to show his feelings.

The next improvement was his increasing ability to talk about his mother and stepfather. (It was a very long time before he could even mention his grandmother, and it was always difficult to know how much he actually remembered of her.) He confided to his house-mother that Daddy was nasty to him and called him bad names. Mummy copied him, only she was nastier than Daddy and used a big stick to hit him with. The house-mother explored whether he felt it was his fault that they were nasty to him. His expression implied that he felt some guilt and then he asked: 'Is it naughty not to like people?' The house-mother replied that it can be very difficult to like everyone. On this occasion, George broke off the conversation, but several times later he asked: 'If my Mummy and Daddy don't want me, should I want them?' He also frequently looked at a family photograph in which he was only too clearly the outsider, standing a little way off from the rest. Brenda was able to use this photograph to talk to George about his parents; she explained that his mother had only a little love to give and it just wasn't enough to go round everyone in the family. He seemed able to understand and accept this and became more comfortable and confident in accepting his own feelings of anger and rejection, though he was often moody and depressed as he worked through his sense of loss, and he needed to talk about his mother and stepfather a lot.

It was some time before he was able to establish a sustained, trusting relationship with his house-mother in which he felt free to test out in a normal way. With other children he had problems too, and the psychiatrist noted that he seemed to feel 'odd man out' and often came off worst in peer group conflicts. Constant effort was needed to build up George's self-confidence, as even a frown or look of surprise could be enough to make him back down from a situation. Gradually he improved so that he could tell a new staff member: 'I'm not going to do what you tell me. You've only just started.' A gently teasing relationship with one of the men on the staff helped him to release some aggression in an appropriate manner and to hold his own better in a group.

As expected, George regressed in toilet training. He wet the bed for a while and had occasional accidents during the day. These lapses were accepted without fuss and did not last long. He also showed interest in matches and fires, and this was dealt with by giving him opportunities to use matches to light candles and to help with bonfires in the garden. Direct psychiatric help was not necessary, but he was seen by the psychiatrist every six months for follow-up and evaluation.

Within a year he had become much happier, relaxed and confident, and though he still had some difficulties with other children he was now accepted by them and able to play constructively. With adults he was discriminating, but had a warm relationship with several staff members, and particularly with his special house-mother. His reading skills improved, though he still lacked concentration at times and was not fully working up to his good potential.

Everyone agreed that George was ready for a new family, and he was asking for this himself. It took much too long, nearly a year, before the right family was found, and this proved to be a very difficult time. George began to give up hope and it was hard to sustain his momentum for growth. His placement went smoothly, but then he had a mild period of regression, during which the new family needed to draw on our experience of dealing with George in his early days at St Luke's. After this he settled very well and his new parents found him a most lovable and rewarding youngster.

6

Planning for Family Placement

The decision to seek a new family for a child in the Long-Stay Unit was always taken at a review conference. Reviews were held at three- or six-monthly intervals and at these future plans were made, reconsidered and revised as necessary. Recommendations for action were then agreed. As regards long-term placement, there were three main alternatives to be thought about: rehabilitation to natural family, transfer to another residential establishment, or placement in a substitute family. Because of the particular kind of children referred to the Unit, return home was only occasionally possible, and a move on to another form of group care was less often appropriate than family placement. Thus the majority of the children leaving the Long-Stay Unit went into new families, and such a placement was our most usual goal. But a good many reviews might pass before the conference could agree that a child was ready to join a new family and, although such a placement might be the agreed long-term plan, it often happened that the short-term decision was 'remain at St Luke's'.

Thus, at the first review on Valerie (aged five at admission) the psychiatric report made a guarded reference to the possibility of family placement: 'There may be some families who would welcome her attractive, intelligent personality and prefer a child who was not seeking a close, demanding, emotional relationship.' Three months later Bill Murcer's report said: 'Relationships are still the area that causes most concern ... but we would be prepared to say that she is really a sensitive girl underneath the façade that we see at present ... Valerie still has a long way to go but I am confident that, if we could find a couple who would be prepared to wait until she

67

held up the olive branch, then it would be a rewarding experience for all involved.'

Six months later still, Brenda Murcer reported to the review conference: 'Valerie continues to try to be independent, self-sufficient and strong-willed but is beginning to verbalize her feelings. She appears to be letting down her defences at times but is still not really trusting adults. She expects them to break promises. Valerie continues to impress us as a very bright child and I wonder if she finds this environment sufficiently stimulating intellectually and socially. I am not suggesting that she is ready for placement yet, but I feel that, while she is working through her emotional difficulties, we should perhaps be providing wider social experiences for her.'

By the next review – 18 months after admission – Valerie's special house-mother reported: 'Over the past six months Valerie has reached the point where she can openly display her affection toward all the staff and has dropped her 'pseudo-tough-guy' attitude ... We feel that she is ready for placement and needs the stable environment that it would provide. Because of Valerie's previous attitudes, we think the new mother will have to be very patient and accepting of Valerie as she is and allow a relationship between them to grow very slowly, giving Valerie the opportunity to assess and express her needs.' This same review conference also considered a potential family for Valerie and concluded that introductions should proceed.

Before the conference could give the green light to any prospective placement, every aspect of the situation had to be considered.

The child's readiness to accept a new family was of course the central issue. As we gained experience we learned to gauge this with increasing sureness and sensitivity, though it was always a difficult area and one in which team support was essential. The child's behaviour and capacity to make relationships were crucial factors, but evidence that he had achieved some genuine understanding and acceptance of his past was equally important. We learned not to proceed until in some way or another the child had expressed his need for a substitute family and been encouraged to think about the kind of family he would want. Some children could actually put their ideas into words, but others had to be helped and could tell us only indirectly. Thus Mark spoke about his friend's new family when he could not bring himself to discuss his own situation and feelings, and Sheila could not talk openly but was able to write a note for the social worker: 'Dear John, I want a new Mum and Dad. Love from Sheila.'

Sometimes words of any sort were too difficult, and residential and field social workers had to use their intuition to interpret the child's play. Dolls' houses and doll families sometimes proved a valuable medium for interpretive play. Percy, whose house-building play has already been mentioned, showed us when he was ready to move on by the openness of his houses, now built with doors and windows instead of the closed boxes with which he began in his use of the Lego set.

Some children had very definite ideas of the type of parents they wanted. For example, David, aged five, asked John Fitzgerald if he could have a new Mum and Dad. When John asked him what kind of Mum and Dad he would like the boy replied: 'I want a big Dad to have fun with.' In this way David, who can best be described as a lovable rogue, was trying to tell us that he wanted someone who could be strong enough to help him contain some of his anxiety and exuberance which, when heightened, led him into conflict. In fact, David was eventually placed in a family where the man was physically big. This was not the only deciding factor in selecting the family, but it does illustrate the point that children's views should be taken into account in the selection process because they can understand their own needs and can communicate them, if only adults will listen.

Similarly, Martin, aged seven, who previously had been placed with a couple who had a child of their own and were unable to provide the stimulation that he needed, was also able to ask John Fitzgerald for a new Mum and Dad, stipulating that: 'They must be interesting, they must like me, and I don't want any other children.' In his way, he had captured the sadness of his previous situation. He was a bright lad but was not liked by his foster mother, and had eventually found himself in rivalry with the natural son of the family.

The child's needs were our prime consideration, but placement with adoption in mind had to depend on whether the natural parents werc likcly to agree to adoption, and the work necessary to achieve this goal undertaken. Thus, plans for Valerie's placement were held up for several months after the child was ready for a new family because there was doubt about whether her mother would give consent, even though she had no plans to resume Valerie's care and we had a family waiting. At this time – before the Children Act 1975 – courts were seldom willing to dispense with a natural parents' consent if they opposed an adoption application. Because of this we sometimes had to opt for fostering, even though we felt adoption would have met the child's needs more completely.

A more usual cause of delay, however, was lack of a suitable family. This could create very serious problems, as it was difficult to maintain a child in a state of equilibrium and readiness for placement if this was too long in coming. Looking back over conference reports one notices the slightly desperate comments of residential staff, e.g.: 'All in all we feel that Martin is more than ready for fostering and can only hope that one of the families in the pipeline will be suitable for him.' Six months later 'Fostering is now desperately urgent for Martin. He has been waiting for over a year already and I question how long we can hold him at this peak of readiness.'

FINDING FAMILIES

Although John Fitzgerald, as the Unit's social worker, did a good deal of home-finding, the main responsibility for finding families for our children lay with the Society's social work staff in areas within a radius of three-and-a-half hours' travelling time from Balham. This meant that families could be considered if they lived within reach of main transport routes such as British Rail Inter-City Services, motorways, or even an internal airport with scheduled flights to London, even though the actual distance might be anything up to 400 miles from St Luke's. The cost of the journeys involved was met by the Children's Society if necessary. Of course this widened the choice considerably, and helped everyone to adhere to the principle of putting the interests of the child first.

Details of children available for placement were circulated

to all the Society's Area Officers so that they could be borne in mind as potential couples became available. From time to time we also undertook specific recruitment efforts on behalf of particular children. At first we had many reservations about the idea of 'advertising' our children and relied on traditional newspaper advertisements using fictitious names. Later we faced more realistically the urgent need for families, and came to terms with our own attitudes. We realized that only by making the public aware of our children and their need for homes would there be any hope of finding a sufficient number of suitable families. When the first national TV feature to recruit families appeared on Granada's 'World in Action' programme in 1974, a film of St Luke's children was used to set the scene and to help viewers to understand children's need for new families. The programme was the forerunner for the regular features that have since appeared on Granada's 'Reports Action' series. Subsequently one of the Long-Stay Unit children was adopted by a family who responded to the 'World in Action' programme. So we found ourselves influencing and being influenced by changing public and professional opinion, and moved into a much more open style of publicity and public relations.

SELECTING FAMILIES

All the families brought to the Long-Stay Unit's conferences for consideration had already been approved by the Society's adoption panel in terms of their general suitability. The Society's system of home study and approval had grown up during the 1960s on the basis of the need for families for a large number of infants and very young children. Unlike some adoption agencies today, the CECS panel at that time did not select or approve a family for a particular child, and for the St Luke's children this matching process was the responsibility of the case conference.

'Matching' is a term widely used in child care and adoption literature, but it does not convey with any accuracy the process we tried to develop in linking children and their new parents. 'Matching' tends to suggest that it is possible to link older children with families who have identical physical and psychological characteristics. This, in our view, is neither possible nor appropriate. We found the term 'selection' more appropriate to describe a process which considered carefully many factors in the child and the substitute family, but in search of compatibility rather than similarity.

Because the Children's Society is a large national organization with regional and area offices, many of our family placement arrangements had to be planned on the lines of an inter-agency placement. Staff in different offices did not always know one another; many of the social workers outside the London area were unfamiliar with St Luke's, our work or our philosophy. Often there was no basis of previous shared placement experience to build on. Mutual trust always had to be developed as we went along, but we did establish some essential ground rules to aid this process.

When one of the Society's social workers had an approved family who, they thought, might be suitable for a child at St Luke's, they sent fairly full details for consideration by the St Luke's team. A 'paper' assessment was made by senior field and residential social workers to see if there were any obvious factors which would make the home unsuitable for that particular child. If the combination looked hopeful, the next step forward was always a face-to-face meeting between the Unit's fieldworker and the family's social worker. The purpose of this meeting was threefold:

1 To continue the process of assessing the appropriateness of the proposed linking.
2 To make arrangements for the Unit's fieldworker to meet the family and the family's social worker to meet the child.
3 To establish a working relationship between the social workers, clarifying areas of responsibility, identifying any differing expectations and sharing points of particular concern.

Inter-agency or inter-area placements inevitably create anxiety. One has to learn to trust other people's work and judgement. We quickly found that the best basis for collaboration was to focus on the child and family under consideration rather than testing out one's colleague's reliability. We also learned the necessity of accepting other people's home studies at face value and not trying to do the study over again according to one's own ideas! However, we found that there was still a lot of work to be done with the families, and the Unit social worker had an important role to play in selection and preparation.

During the initial assessment, the family's social worker would have considered with them some of the pleasures and problems invariably involved in taking on an older child, but this could be done only in very general terms. At that time there was rather less stress on preparation for prospective substitute parents than there is today and, in any case, the wide geographical scatter of the families would have made group discussion or training sessions virtually impossible. So the preparation usually had to be done as part of the introduciton and placement process. It started with a joint visit to the family by the Unit's fieldworker and the family's own local social worker.

The primary purpose of the visit was to explore in detail factors that would have a bearing on the suitability of this family for the particular child under consideration. This involved assessing their understanding and sensitivity to the child's experiences and problems and their willingness to work closely with the staff in helping the child to move. Other topics which we always covered were their motivation to adopt an older and deprived child, their expectations, life-style and family roles. It was also important to think about practical matters such as availability of suitable schooling or any special services which this child was likely to need. It may be helpful to look at each of these topics in some detail.

Motivation

A family's basic motivation is always a central issue in an adoption assessment. When placement of an older child is being considered, this takes on an extra dimension. How does this motivation affect their flexibility? Is this a family which can appropriately be asked to stretch their ideas about the kind of child they could accept, or is their overriding need for a baby?

The case of Mr and Mrs D. provides a useful illustration of this point. Mr and Mrs D. had been approved as foster parents with a view to adoption for a mixed-race baby, but in discussion with their social worker they had indicated that they could accept an older child into their home. Their application had been forwarded to St Luke's and at first sight it seemed they might be just what we were needing for one of our mixed-race boys. However, during the discussion with the Unit's social worker, the couple showed little or no enthusiasm for taking such a child, and in view of this we suggested that they give further consideration to the question of the age of the child ' they could accept. The following day they contacted their social worker to say they now realized that they really only wanted a baby.

Mr and Mrs B. on the other hand, ultimately presented a very different picture. They had originally written in with a fairly stereotyped request to adopt a baby. Later they stretched their thinking and their application was sent to St Luke's. When they were interviewed by the Unit's social worker it was found that they had been married for a number of years, were in their early forties and childless. Both appeared to have a genuine wish for a family and there seemed no doubt that they would provide a great deal of warmth and love, irrespective of a child's age. Although they had a strong emotional need for a child, they also showed a high degree of sensitivity and a willingness to attempt to control their own needs until a child was ready to make its own response. In his article 'A Systematic Approach to Selecting Foster Parents', Neil Kay commented on this aspect of motivation: 'An emotionally mature foster mother will not eliminate her need, but will be able to have a degree of control over it. She will be able to accept that the need which brings her to fostering will only be partly filled part of the time.'[1]

In attempting to define a family's pattern of motivation and decide whether or not it is compatible with the needs of a specific child, one is searching not for perfection but for mutuality. If what the child and family can offer each other fits their particular needs, then a close, firm bond is likely. But if their needs are incompatible, disappointment and failure will almost inevitably result.

Emotional expectations

Inevitably, substitute parents all have their own expectations of the emotional response which they hope to receive from any child that may be placed with them. This will vary in intensity from one family to another. Such expectation is, of course, allied to motivation and, during assessment interviews, the social worker must attempt to define the degree and type of emotional return that the prospective parents hope to receive. It was the Unit social worker's responsibility to elicit this information and consider it in relation to specific children.

Perhaps this point can best be illustrated by once more using the case of Philip as an example. Philip was five at the point where a substitute family was required for him. His early life had been traumatic. Prior to his arrival at St Luke's he had had two periods living with his natural mother, and on the last occasion had been subjected to a great deal of physical and emotional ill-treatment. Although during his stay at St Luke's Philip had become more secure emotionally, he remained somewhat of an introvert, did not easily make relationships, and became withdrawn when demonstrative demands were made upon him.

Two approved families were considered as possibilities for Philip. In the course of the interviews it became clear that Mr and Mrs G. were expecting a quick and overt emotional return from any child placed with them. Mr and Mrs Z., on the other hand, certainly hoped for an emotional return from a child, but were not themselves highly demonstrative. Mr and Mrs G.'s expectations of a swift affectionate response was likely to work against a successful placement for Philip, while Mr and Mrs Z.'s much more contained emotional style was seen as a positive factor which would be helpful to Philip if he were to be placed with them.

It should be emphasized at this point that this factor was seen to be mitigating against the placement only of this particular child with Mr and Mrs G., and did not make them unsuitable as a prospective new family. On the contrary, a child who had a different pattern of emotional response, and who would enjoy overt demonstrations of love from a substitute family, would benefit from what the Gs had to offer as well as meeting their own needs.

Intellectual expectations

In his preliminary discussion with prospective families, the Unit social worker sought to assess and define the intellectual capacity of the family, and the degree of stimulation to which a child would be exposed. This had to be considered in relation to the needs of the specific children for whom we were seeking families. Some children needing placement are intellectually limited, and many more are educationally retarded and not achieving anything like their full potential, so it is essential to make sure that a prospective family does not have unrealistic expectations or subject the child to undue pressure. Nevertheless, we felt it equally important to look for adequate stimulation and to try and ensure that a child's intellectual needs would be met.

This point is very clearly illustrated by Martin, the boy referred to earlier in this chapter, who wanted his new parents to be 'interesting'. Martin had an IQ score of 127. During his stay at St Luke's he had needed a great deal of stimulation and was able to develop his intellectual ability with enthusiasm, although his emotional problems had limited his attainments so far. Our aim was to place him with a couple who could meet his long-term intellectual needs without being unrealistic about his current attainments.

It would have been easy to take the view either that a family with modest intellectual expectations would be the most appropriate in view of Martin's limited attainments, or that this factor should not be considered important in view of the child's other needs and the reality that, because he was of mixed racial background, the choice of families for him was likely to be limited. We did not take this view, but felt that it was necessary to find parents with the intellectual capacity to keep up with this child's sharp mind and the academic background to help him make the most of his innate ability. We were confident that with sensitive help and stimulation his intellectual potential could be realized, but felt that if he was pressured into reaching for unrealistic targets the effect would be at the very least unhelpful and might even prevent him from reaching anywhere near his full capacity.

With this very much in mind, Mr and Mrs C. were interviewed. Both of them had a university education, both had developed their careers in the academic world, and yet they had retained a deep appreciation of the way in which their respective families had provided them with an opportunity without pressuring them in any way. During lengthy discussions it became clear that they could provide a relaxed as well as an intellectually stimulating environment. Martin was placed and did extremely well.

Life-style and individual roles
It is not difficult to appreciate the importance of life-style when considering placement of an older child. It is obviously expecting a lot from both sides if a child who does not like sport is placed with a madly sporty family. However, it is not alway easy in an inter-agency placement to get a clear picture of the way a family lives. How often, for example, are substitute families described as 'outgoing' or 'home-loving'? These terms are vague as well as subjective, and give little clue to the life-style which the family actually enjoys. It was often a task for the Unit's social worker to attempt to define such terms more clearly. Did the adjective 'outgoing' refer to interest in sport and the outdoor life or to a busy social life with friends or clubs? Did it mean a commitment to community or church activities or large involvement in local committees, or did it refer only to interpersonal relationships? Furthermore, we needed to know whether these activities were undertaken as a family or if each family member had separate interests. Above all we had to consider how the family would adjust to admit a newcomer to the group and whether there was a child in the Long-Stay Unit who would benefit and fit in with that way of living.

Part of the family's life-style will, of course, be dependent upon the role which each individual is allocated. Because children in the Long-Stay Unit had all been subjected to a number of severe rejections, the 'role set' of a prospective family had to be carefully considered in the light of the child's individual needs. It was not a question of making value judgements but of clarification and genuine understanding of a variety of ways of relating.

When Anthony – whose treatment at St Luke's has been described in chapter 5 – was ready for a new family, it was particularly necessary to pay attention to the current and probable future roles of potential parents. Anthony had suffered a great deal in his previous foster family, in which the husband adopted a negative uninvolved role while the wife was domineering and over-controlling. Anthony experienced her as a dominating, but negative mother figure. In assessing whether a couple could meet Anthony's needs, the Unit's social worker had to try and weigh up whether they could demonstrate positive, traditional mother and father roles and clear-cut masculine and feminine characteristics. For some children this would not have mattered much, but for this particular child it was seen as an important continuation of the treatment and restorative experiences he had benefited from at St Luke's.

Family structure and physical surroundings

The presence or absence of other children in the family is an obvious factor in assessing its suitability for a particular child. Some youngsters had had previous experiences which made it particularly desirable or undesirable for them to have siblings close in age or older or younger or the same sex or the opposite sex. Less usual, but also potentially important, is the presence of a grandparent in the household. For some children a grandparent will be an important added bonus and a very special person. In other situations there could be unhelpful overtones from the past or too much opportunity for playing adults off against each other.

The type of house a family lives in may appear quite unimportant but in a particular instance it may be very relevant, and questions of town or country or the racial mix or cultural climate of the community may need consideration. The quality of educational facilities in the area always merits attention because such matters as the size of classes, teaching methods used, and the attitudes of teaching staff to foster children will affect all children and might be of major importance in some instances.

The case of Anthony illustrates the importance of detail in making decisions about linking children and families. Mr and Mrs H. were referred to the Long-Stay Unit as a potentially suitable family for Tony but, when they were interviewed in their own home, three aspects became evident which had a marked similarity with this little boy's previous unsuccessful placement:

1   The Hs lived in a similar, stone built, semi-detached Victorian-style house.
2   Their motivation was rather the same in that, like the previous foster parents, they had experienced the tragedy of losing a child through death due to a congenital heart condition.
3   The wife's mother lived in the house with them.

Taken individually these factors need not have been a contra-indication to placement, but taken collectively the risks involved were trebled. Anthony had at this point just worked through the difficulties from his past placement, and to link him with Mr and Mrs H. would have involved a serious possibility of resurrecting inappropriate anxiety. We feared that Mr and Mrs H. would find themselves in an acute transference situation which they might not have been able to handle, and there was every likelihood of a damaging counter-transference developing. The St Luke's team were agreed that, *in this instance*, the suggested placement constituted too great a risk. In other circumstances, or with just one factor involved, the decision might well have been different. Every new family placement involves risk, and sometimes even major risks are justified. What has to be avoided is failure to recognize risks through lack of detailed and accurate information about the child and the prospective family, or failure to appreciate the significance of certain factors or combinations of factors.

Ability to collaborate with the agency
The methods and techniques used in the introduction of a child to a substitute family and the establishment of the relationship are dealt with in detail in the next chapter. However, before selecting a family to link with a specific child, we thought it was vital to tell them about the work of the Long-Stay Unit and try to explain the methods used in an introduction and in supporting the subsequent placement. It was part of the function of the Unit's social worker to discuss these matters with each family during the joint visit made with their local

social worker. This provided an opportunity to ask questions and air doubts and disagreements before deciding about proceeding further.

We found that few families completely accepted our point of view at this stage. What was important was their ability to see some value in the work of the Unit and the methods and techniques we used. We looked for evidence of the beginning of a working relationship, for without this the linking of a child with a couple is likely to be traumatic at best and may well prove unsuccessful. The contrasting attitudes of two families highlight this particular point. At their meeting with the Unit social worker, Mr and Mrs J. could see no value in the work that had been attempted or was about to be attempted in the introduction of a particular child to a new family. Mrs J. in particular, thought that the Unit's methods were irrelevant and that the systematic and analytical approach we used had little value. 'I think intuition is best', she said. In view of the fact that this couple had no confidence in the way in which St Luke's operated, there seemed little point in attempting to link the Js with one of our children – a view also arrived at by the couple themselves.

Mr and Mrs Z., mentioned earlier in this chapter, also had firm views at first on the methods and techniques we used. Mrs Z., in fact, described psychology as rubbish. (The term psychology was not used by the Unit social worker, but was her interpretation òf what had been said.) However, after lengthy discussion of the subject, Mr and Mrs Z., although still not in complete agreement with the social worker, could genuinely accept the reasoning behind the ideas being put forward. They proved able to work with us in a collaborative way.

Social workers as well as families sometimes found our ideas difficult to accept. One accused us of 'slavish adherence to one method' and urged us to press ahead to place the child regardless, pointing out that 'there are not many couples prepared to accept these children'. For our part we did not consider that we had one rigid method. We tried to use a broad framework, in which the guiding principle was that the needs of the child must be put first. But we did feel strongly that, if a proposed family proved to have little or no sympathy for our approach or methods, then this lack of mutual confidence would certainly be communicated to the child, setting up all sorts of conflicts and probably sabotaging the placement.

MAKING DECISIONS

After meeting the family and a discussion with their local social worker, the Unit's fieldworker produced a full report, which he discussed with senior residential staff. If all felt that this family seemed to offer the kind of home a specific child needed, the report and recommendation were submitted to a case conference. In addition to the usual conference group, the family's social worker and his or her Area Officer would also attend.

The conference would review the child's progress and discuss in detail the report and recommendation from the Unit's fieldworker. Each query would be fully explored so that every conceivable problem could be considered. The object was to enable doubts and difficulties to be expressed, not hidden or overlooked, and only when the conference was in agreement with the recommendation would the next step be taken.

Of course some doubts and anxieties remained, even with this careful procedure. No one can know another person or family completely, let alone predict with any accuracy the 'chemistry' of an artificially created family unit. Often the St Luke's team were confronted by the inevitable limitations of availability of suitable homes. Like other agencies, we found that homes for disturbed and deprived school-age children were in short supply. In this situation it is easy to submit to external and internal pressure to place a child with a family because it is approved and available, rather than because it is the right home for the particular child. The team constantly faced the problem of a child needing substitute family care, but nothing really suitable being immediately available. This, however, was when the team approach of the Unit was particularly effective. If one member of the team, because of his anxiety to get a child into a family setting, wanted to rush into selecting a couple for the wrong reasons, the group could act as a modifying influence to prevent an inappropriate placement.

This was something that every member of the team had to face at some time because of the commitment each of us had to ensure that the plans made for a child were implemented. It was particularly difficult when a child frequently asked when he was going to get a new family. Having to keep repeating: 'We have not found the right family yet, but we are still looking', makes it difficult for an individual to resist pressure to select hastily. When a whole team is involved, it becomes easier for the individual to remain firm to the guiding principle of putting the child first.

Sometimes colleagues complained that St Luke's staff were too fussy in the selection of substitute parents. We argued that the object was to do everything possible to select the right placement for each child in our care. Nevertheless, we recognized that an individual can become over-identified with a particular child or 'hung-up' on the type of home needed so that however many potentially appropriate families are suggested, all are rejected as having some flaws. When this happened, the team influence could again provide a corrective balance and enable the individual concerned to see what was happening.

7

Introductions between Children and Families

There is a good deal of disagreement among social workers about how best to introduce a child to a new family. Placement theory emphasizes that introductions of children to new families should be gradual, without pressure on either side to precipitate a decision. But what constitutes a gradual introduction? In practice this seems to be anything from one contact between the child and new parents to a series of meetings and visits stretching over many months. So often the style and the pace of the meeting have been dictated by practical necessity. Busy generic social workers struggling with a large and varied caseload may think they cannot afford the luxury of full participation in placement. Residential social workers can be so pressured by staff shortages that they feel they just cannot give the necessary time to this aspect of their work. Because introductions are somewhat time-consuming, there is a temptation to skimp, take short cuts or opt out. But short cuts can be dangerous.

The St Luke's team was particularly aware of the dangers of lack of preplacement work and hurried introductions because so many of our children had experienced foster or adoption home breakdowns, and with the benefit of hindsight we could see how inadequate preparation had been a contributory factor in these failures. In the very early days of the Unit, we had also had an experience in which Brenda Murcer stifled her qualms about a proposed placement and agreed to a child going on a long introductory 'holiday' with a family he had met only twice. It was a disaster. Though the child recovered rather quickly, the family were deeply distressed.

With these sad examples very much in mind, we tried to develop a framework for introductions which would meet the needs of children and families. Of course the framework could not be rigid. We had to adapt flexibly and often 'play it by ear' for each situation. Much would depend on the age, personality and previous experiences of the child. The personalities of the prospective new parents, their other family commitments and the distance between their home and St Luke's all had a bearing on what was feasible and appropriate. But in every case we felt that certain objectives could be identified and certain aims met.

For the sake of clarity, one can divide the introduction programme into three parts: preparation; first meeting; subsequent meetings. In reality there was a lot of overlap, as preparation continued right on into placement and what could be achieved at first or subsequent meetings varied from child to child. Thus Cathy, who was of the same mixed racial background as her prospective new family, walked into a room full of strangers (her prospective new parents and a number of their relatives), sat herself on her new mother's lap, beamed at the assembled company and said: 'My new Mummy'. Although only four she clearly recognized their similarity to herself and felt immediately at ease. Her placement moved ahead very swiftly. By contrast Polly, near the same age but of different personality, was so anxious about new people that it took several visits before she could as much as venture outside the garden gate for a picnic with her prospective parents. Some families arrived at St Luke's quite secure in their decision that the child described to them would be joining their family. Others had to make several 'first visits' before their anxiety subsided to a level where they could hope to make a rational decision about whether or not to go ahead.

PREPARATION

The preparation of the child started from the time it was decided in conference that substitute family care should be the goal of treatment. By the time a linking plan had been made the child was always as fully prepared as possible in general terms. The final stages of preparation for placement would only be possible once introductions were well under way.

Work with the families had a different rhythm. Although we hoped and expected that preparation would have begun right from the start of the assessment, this could be only in general terms until a specific child was proposed. From that moment on the pace of preparation quickened, feelings became increasingly involved and the working relationship between the family and the Society took on a new dimension.

Whenever possible, the family's social worker visited the Long-Stay Unit several times and became well acquainted with the child to be placed, so that he or she could discuss the child with the family on the basis of first-hand knowledge. When the local social worker was unable or unwilling to become this closely involved, the Unit's social worker had to take on responsibility for detailed discussion of the child with the family.

Whichever social worker undertook it, the task was to bring to the prospective substitute family a lively and realistic picture of the child. Families were given as much information as possible about the child's natural parents, the reason why he was in the agency's care, his history since admission – including any moves that had occurred and the reasons why they were necessary – the purpose of admitting him to Balham, his progress with us and his current situation, such as school achievements, interests and hobbies. Dealing with general factual information such as this is relatively straightforward. Much more demanding is the task of discussing the child in terms of his personality, problems and needs. It is these areas that make it essential for the person conveying the information to have first-hand knowledge of the child.

To provide a living word picture of a child's personality, one has to move beyond such well-worn phrases as 'an outgoing boy with a sense of humour'. After all, what does 'outgoing' mean in this context? What is a 'sense of humour', bearing in mind that humour has many varied forms? We found that our description of a child's personality was much more vivid and realistic when it included one or two anecdotes to use as illustrations and was allied to a physical description of the child. Photographs also helped a lot.

We found that, in discussing the child's problems or explaining difficulties which new parents would have to cope with, we had to define our terms very clearly. It is not enough to say that a child's difficult behaviour is caused by insecurity stemming from a previous experience. This sort of generalization is quite useless to prospective parents who are wondering how to manage the behaviour problem. We tried to explain clearly what the difficulty was, how it manifested itself, what previous experiences seemed to be the basic cause of the current problem and how we thought it could best be dealt with. During the preparatory stages we found it helpful to sit down with the prospective parents and look at the specific needs of the child, making sure that our definition of terms was clear and avoiding jargon and well-worn phrases. It is so easy to fall into the trap of generalities and define a child's needs as 'a loving, sensitive substitute family', etc. We tried to be very explicit about the child's way of relating to people, to explain whether or not we thought he was going to be able to cope with open expression of affection and whether he would be looking to one parent figure as opposed to the other for emotional support or physical affection. We found that the word 'sensitive' in this context was inappropriate and could cause confusion. Some couples initially construed the word as meaning little or no discipline, and we soon realized that it was always necessary to make sure that people understood exactly what we meant.

Discussion of the child's usual way of responding led quite naturally to talking about why we thought that the couple could meet the needs of this particular child. We tried to be totally honest and open and give them enough information to enable them to decide whether or not to move on to the next stage, which was a visit to Balham for a further discussion with the residential staff and perhaps a glimpse of the child. In view of the importance and significance of the discussion that had taken place and the highly emotional content of the information, it was hardly surprising that people quite often wanted time to think about taking this next step. Sometimes they would ask for a further discussion with their own social worker before proceeding. Occasionally they decided that the child suggested was not the right one for them or that they could not cope with his problems. One family, for instance, decided that the child we had described was just too dark in colour. They had been prepared for a mixed-race child but not, apparently, for a boy who looked black.

It has been suggested to us that no one could possibly assimilate the amount of information that we gave in one interview. This is true, but it was not intended that they should. We hoped that they would take from the discussion what they considered important, and during the following weeks the Unit staff would have opportunities to reinforce the content of this interview. We found that, as the introduction and placement proceeded, our substitute families were able to draw on the intensive preparatory discussions. We came to realize that the interview marked the beginning of a crucial stage in the process in which the new family would be attempting to learn as much as possible from every source about the child for whom they hoped to provide a future. As they built up a picture of the child and his needs, they were able to weigh up their own resources, strengths and weaknesses and take an active share in the planning and decisions. We tried to treat them as partners rather than clients, even while we recognized that they might need a great deal of support during what was inevitably an anxious time.

Another essential element of the preparatory work with the family was to set out in detail our philosophy of placement and a general outline for the introduction. The joint interview of local social worker and Unit fieldworker began to demonstrate our team approach, and this was continued during visits to Balham, when residential staff played a major part in discussions, information giving and support. The aim was to enable prospective parents to become part of the team of people working together on behalf of the child.

THE FIRST MEETING

If the preparatory period had gone according to plan, the first meeting between family and child slotted into place as one more step in the introduction process rather than a big climax. In fact we learned to restrict our own expectation of this occasion to a very modest level and tried to help the prospective parents to do the same.

The usual plan was to arrange a casual, purely social encounter with the child during the prospective family's first visit to Balham. But though this encounter was no doubt the highlight, we saw the whole visit as an opportunity to fulfil three other aims:

1   To provide an opportunity for prospective parents to clarify and test out what they had already learned about the child by discussing him with his care givers.
2   To demonstrate the team approach of the staff. (The family's own social worker was usually present also.)
3   To reinforce what had already been said about the importance of a carefully controlled introductory period and discuss just how family, child and staff would be working together.

We also used this opportunity to establish the question of names and how the child was to refer to his prospective parents while he was getting to know them.

One girl in the Long-Stay Unit had previously experienced an introduction during which a couple were introduced to her as her new Mum and Dad the first time they met. After two more visits Valerie went to live with them. She did not settle from the beginning and eventually the placement broke down in bitter and angry circumstances. It was many months after coming to us before Valerie could talk about her experiences. Eventually, however, she told Brenda Murcer that she had not liked the adopters from the first time they met. When asked why she did not explain how she felt to a member of staff in the previous establishment, she replied: 'No one asked me.' Introducing the couple as Mum and Dad from the outset symbolized the way in which the staff involved had committed Valerie to a relationship for which she was not ready. Her anxiety level was raised to such a pitch that it became impossible for her to put her feelings into words. The end result was a highly disturbed child whose ability to relate to adults was impaired to such a degree that her introduction to a second substitute family two-and-a-half years later had to be handled very carefully indeed.

We found it best to encourage people to use their Christian names until such time as the child chose the more affectionate terms he would like to use. This was usually very acceptable and worked out well.

Each meeting was planned to be as gentle and easy as possible but there was no standard pattern. We wanted from the first to establish with the substitute family the principle of moving *at the child's pace*, which was a recurring theme in the work of the unit.

When Mr and Mrs F. visited for the first time to meet Anthony, he and some of the other children were begging to clean John Fitzgerald's car – mainly because it was a very hot day and they wanted to play with the hose. Eventually John agreed and the task was begun. Before very long, all the children joined in, plus the staff and Mr and Mrs F. With all the manpower (not to mention child power) involved, the car should have sparkled. Sad to relate, it was dirtier when finished than at the beginning! However, the activity created a great deal of discussion and comment between children and adults and gave Mr and Mrs F. a chance to see Anthony in a relaxed, informal setting and to form their own initial impression of him.

Martin, aged eight, was a part West Indian boy who very enthusiastically started to learn to play the recorder and had insisted that he should practise it every evening with Brenda Murcer before going to bed. One evening, Brenda told him it would have to be a short practice because some people were coming to see her. After about twenty minutes, Mr and Mrs C. arrived. Martin usually became very anxious when confronted by strangers but on this occasion was surprisingly relaxed for him, and chatted about prehistoric animals until it was time to go to bed.

So, for Anthony and Martin there were two different types of initial contact, each happening in as natural a way as possible. There were many others, but the important point was to ensure that we, as staff, did not in any way indicate that the couple's visit was anything special. This was not as difficult as it sounds because a continual stream of visitors came to Balham and this visit would not necessarily be different from any other. It would be foolish to suggest, however, that children never guessed the reality of the situation as, obviously, in a setting like Balham, where most children are being helped towards a subsequent placement, they will be aware of the possibility of a couple visiting the centre in order to meet them. We were often asked why, if this was the case, we bothered to try to arrange a casual first contact. The answer to this lay in the two interdependent elements that were of vital importance in this first meeting – its function and the anxiety level of the participants. In our view, the function was simply to provide an introduction between a child and two adults in a social context, nothing else. There was no commitment on either side, no meaningful relationship, just a social contact. In not attempting to achieve anything further, the child's anxiety was not raised to an unacceptable level and the prospective parents had a chance to see him acting in a normal manner.

This style of introduction was not just for the benefit of the child. The first encounter also provoked many anxieties within prospective substitute families. Their first trip to Balham was likely to be their first visit to a residential establishment. They would therefore be in a totally unfamiliar setting and, since a children's home often arouses unexpectedly strong feelings, they would often have to cope with the emotional turmoil of their reactions to the establishment as well as to the child. We began to appreciate all this more clearly as a result of our experience with a family who subsequently successfully provided a home for a boy from the Long-Stay Unit, but found their first encounter with him particularly difficult. Mrs F., who was normally relatively placid, was so anxious that she could not stop talking in a high-pitched, shrill voice, and certainly she was in no frame of mind to establish anything other than an initial social contact. We were thankful that nothing more than this had been planned!

Mrs F. reinforced for us the importance of recognizing and acknowledging the anxieties that can exist for the child and family. It is no good attempting to achieve more than is realistically within the capabilities of the individuals involved. However, the anxieties of substitute families on these occasions did provide an opportunity for our staff to help them verbalize their feelings, and thus begin the process that would help them eventually to feel part of the team that was working with the child. Before they left the centre, a brief discussion would take place in which we suggested they should go home, think about the day's experiences and their reaction to the child and then decide whether they wanted to proceed. Following this contact, their own social worker would visit to help them analyse their thoughts and feelings and, if appropriate, arrange a tentative date for a second visit to Balham.

SUBSEQUENT MEETINGS

Plans for subsequent meetings had to find a balance between the needs of the child and the personal circumstances of the family. In essence this meant that the way the contacts developed depended on the child, but the frequency of the contacts was determined by the prospective parents, although of course these two elements interacted.

The first chapter of this book described how the long-term therapeutic work of the Unit developed from our efforts to meet the needs of three-year-old Polly, and her treatment was discussed in chapter 5. She also taught us a lot about introductions.

During her preparation for placement we had learned that it was vital to let the pace be determined by Polly's readiness to proceed to the next phase. This proved to be equally important as we progressed through the stages of introduction and placement. The pace had to be geared to her ability to cope with what was going on. Inevitably we made mistakes, but as usual Polly made them obvious to us and quick thinking or reviewing the situation enabled us to proceed with an enlightened awareness of the support which she needed. An example of this occurred during the third visit of Polly's prospective family. With Polly's agreement we had arranged for them to take her for a picnic on the common. She had picnicked there before so the place was familiar, but when the time came she became anxious and refused to go. Of course we should have anticipated her need for a familiar person to give her a sense of security whilst away from the Unit with adults whom she had not yet learned to trust. It was too much to expect her to get into a car and be driven away by these people. The picnic site was changed to the front lawn, the front door was left open and Brenda popped out from time to time to reassure her that all was under control. At the end of the meal Brenda joined them for a chat. The conversation was brought round to the fact that Polly would soon be old enough to start school. A short car ride to see the local school was suggested. First Polly, Brenda and the prospective foster mother went. Then Brenda stayed behind while both foster parents and Polly went and returned safely to the centre.

This experience obviously helped Polly, as during the family's next visit she felt able to go with them to the common for a picnic. It also helped us to be more aware of the way anxiety can cause a child to regress very rapidly to earlier defensive behaviour.

Two further examples may help to illustrate a varied approach based on detailed knowledge of the child's history, personality and usual response to new situations.

The physical and psychological ill-treatment which Philip had suffered before he came to the Long-Stay Unit meant that his first positive experience of adults – in particular women – was with the staff at Balham, and everyone outside the Unit was treated with the utmost suspicion.

We recognized that before Philip would be able to relate to prospective parents, they would have to become part of Balham. We therefore arranged for Mrs Z. to visit the centre in the guise of a volunteer for two afternoons a week, with Mr Z. collecting his wife after he had finished work for the day. At no point did we try to engineer contact between Philip and the Zs, but just waited for him to see them as familiar figures. Gradually, over a period of three months, he began to make contact with them. It was little things at first, but as he became more sure of himself, he began to search them out and to involve them in his activities.

During this period, Philip's house-mother – with whom he had a strong relationship – continued to help him to think about his future and, when he brought up the subject of Mr and Mrs Z., she listened and indicated that it was safe to express his feelings. At this stage the feed-back from the house-mother was our only realiable means of understanding how Philip viewed those prospective parents whom as yet he knew only as friends. If we had relied upon the child's behaviour towards them we could have been easily misled, because outwardly he appeared disinterested for long periods. We knew, however, that every new person who came into Philip's world he would treat in similar fashion. We had selected Mr and Mrs Z. as being a couple we thought capable of meeting this child's needs in the long term, but all we could do at that point in time was to wait patiently to see if Philip would eventually agree. One cannot over-emphasize the importance of continuous feed-back from all members of staff in such situations. If it had not been for the house-mother's reports of Philip's increasing interest and involvement, we might have abandoned the plan. As it was, by the end of the three months, Philip had progressed to a point where he was making short trips away from the centre with Mr and Mrs Z., and shortly after this he started visiting their home.

Anthony – whom by this time readers will know quite well – was equally emotionally vulnerable, having experienced a painful fostering breakdown. But whereas Philip reacted with aloof suspicion of strangers, Anthony was a different personality and covered his anxiety with a boisterous and apparently outgoing manner. He quickly became interested in the visits of his prospective foster parents, but they had a 250-mile round trip each time they came to Balham, and to begin with felt they could come only every two weeks.

Anthony soon realized that Mr and Mrs F. were coming specially to see him. Not surprisingly, in view of his difficulties with his former foster mother, he identified more quickly with Mr F. than with his wife. On their third visit Tony asked if they could come again the next weekend and they agreed. Unfortunately a family crisis made this impossible. They wrote to Tony to tell him what had happened and his house-mother did her best to explain, but it was obvious that he was not accepting these reasons very readily.

When the Fs arrived for their next visit we explained that Mrs F. in particular might find that Tony needed to reject her at first. We all went into the garden. At first Tony pretended not to notice us but after a while he walked over and chatted to Mr F. but completely ignored Mrs F. He then wandered off to the sand-pit to play on his own. As John Fitzgerald and Mrs F. walked over to the sand-pit Tony shouted: 'Go home.' He then went to play in a wooden cabin at one end of the garden, and when Mrs F. approached a little later he said aggressively: 'I am going to lock you in.' Mrs F. light-heartedly said that she didn't mind, and Tony made a great play of locking her in the cabin until a group of other children joined in. At this point he decided vehemently to rescue her and shouted angrily at the children to stop. Taking hold of Mrs F.'s hand, he led her away from the cabin and then asked her why she had not visited when she said she would. Mrs F. explained again and this time Tony accepted it. In view of what had happened, we asked the Fs if they could visit more frequently for the next few weeks and they readily agreed, despite the distance they had to travel. They arranged to come again in three days' time and there was no doubt that Tony spent an anxious three days until Mr and Mrs F. reappeared.

In every case, contact between child and family was gradually increased until the child was ready to go out for short periods with his prospective parents. To begin with, a member of staff accompanied the child and family on short trips away, such as a walk to the local park or to the shops. We were often asked why this was necessary. The reason was that at this stage the child was still identifying with Balham and needed reassurance that he would return, the member of staff being that assurance. Once the child felt confident enough to go out on his own, the trips were stepped up to half a day and eventually a full day. With some children this point was reached quite quickly. With others it took much longer.

This period of preliminary contact was important for reasons other than establishing a social relationship between the child and the substitute family. We used the period intensively to reinforce the team approach which we felt was so important. At the end of each contact a member of the Unit's staff would discuss the day's events with the prospective parents so as to understand the interaction of those involved. This helped the couple to feel that they had a contribution to make to the decision about each step. It was also an opportunity to reassure the family that progress had been made, however small. We felt that this was very important. Prospective parents cannot sustain an extended period of visiting unless they understand its purpose very clearly and can see movement toward the goal of placement. Each couple needed to see that there was a point to what was happening, because progress was sometimes slow and there was an ever-present danger of frustration taking over and jeopardizing the situation. Each meeting during an introduction needs to achieve something definite, and it was the social worker's role to set up a plan for the occasion in consultation with the family and child. A major objective was to suggest something which they could do together which, by creating a shared experience and something to talk about, would help to build a communication bridge. Often the children themselves had good ideas, like the boy who wanted to visit the prehistoric monsters museum.

Between each visit it was hoped that the couple's own social worker would be providing additional support, as it often helped to have someone outside Balham to talk to. In the same way the child would have opportunities to discuss his feelings although, of course, he did not always do this in a direct way. Often communication was through a third person or object. This might be a toy or another child, or he might reveal his feelings through play or school activities. Martin provides a good example of this phenomenon. Although the first meeting with his new parents went very easily, during the early stages of introductions Martin seemed quite unable to express his feelings to any member of staff concerned with his placement. He appeared to be quieter than usual and withdrawing from relationships with adults in the Unit. However, he had a special friend within the house, a boy a few months younger, with whom he did discuss his feelings and stated his views of Mr and Mrs C. and their home. The friend passed this information to the house-mother with whom he had a special relationship. The house-mother was thus able to inform the rest of the team that Martin liked Mr and Mrs C. very much, was excited about their visits and hoped he could continue to see them.

Situations of this sort highlight the importance of good communications amongst the staff. Every scrap of information about the feelings of the child and adults was gathered up and communicated to all members of the team, who consulted each other and agreed each step of the way. Establishing this team approach from the beginning paid dividends in the later stages, when anxieties were again heightened. We found that each introductory period had to be treated as a completely new situation and the team approach had to be established with each child and substitute family.

There came a point in every introduction when the child decided that he wanted to see the home where his new friends lived. We did not act on this request without due consideration, even though the first visit often lasted only a few hours and was intended only to be an opportunity for the child to begin to get to know the prospective family home. Just as for the first meeting, expectations of the first visit need to be kept in perspective, otherwise anxiety mounts to an inappropriate level. We found that very careful preparation was essential, but even then quick but sensitive decisions might have to be made to deal with situations as they arose on the day. The child was usually accompanied by a member of staff with whom he had a strong relationship.

Some children asked to go and live with the family before they had even seen their house, and in these situations the member of staff involved always introduced a note of reality by posing questions such as: 'How do you know you will like the food Mrs So-and-So cooks?' or: 'Supposing the beds are lumpy?' This may sound superficial and negative, but it helped the child to think in a practical way about the reality of living with a family. The staff person would then move on to look at the child's feelings, helping him to put into words any anxieties about his relationship with the family, and would suggest that he talked to Bill and Brenda Murcer or John Fitzgerald about a possible day visit. We would then look at dates and discuss the plan with the family, explaining to them what had been said in the discussion with the child so that they could be prepared for questions on subjects like lumpy beds. All this may sound tediously pedantic and time-consuming but we found that the time and effort involved were very worthwhile. It could not, of course, ensure a trouble-free placement, but it did mean that our children had worked through many of their inevitable worries and fears while still supported by familiar people who not only knew them very well indeed but also had the opportunity to consult with one another and pool ideas.

For the child, a first visit to prospective parents can be filled with anxiety and conflict related to his past experience of rejection and his hopes and fears of this new relationship.

Because of these anxieties, it was sometimes necessary for the escort to remain with the child the whole time, suggestions that the escort should leave and return in a couple of hours raising the child's anxiety level quite considerably. Quite often the escort would take along some work and sit in another room. But if the family had not been helped to understand why the escort might have to remain, they could be worried into a state in which they ceased to function adequately. The plan for the day was flexible, for example, the decision as to whether or not the escort remained with the child was always left open.

The process of familiarization was built up over an unspecified number of day visits, the child dictating the number, the objectives and the point where the escort could retire gracefully from the substitute family home. Between visits a considerable amount of time had to be given to communication about what was going on and how everyone concerned felt about it.

Sooner or later the child would ask: 'Can I go to Mr and Mrs —'s house to sleep?' We always used this opportunity to discuss why he wanted to sleep there, how long he would stay and what he hoped would happen. Usually at first the child would stay for one night only and he usually had the security of a telephone number or address where the escort could be contacted. This visit would be followed by others, and the number of nights spent away from Balham built up gradually in consultation with the child and the family.

Escorting arrangements for these overnight stays varied according to the needs of the child, but we did try to adhere to one overriding principle. No matter who escorted the child *from* Balham, the prospective family were never asked to bring him back after an overnight visit. We did not want the new parents to be identified as 'bringing back' or 'rejecting' parents. On the few occasions when substitute families returned children after an overnight stay we found it was a painful, rejecting experience for both sides and one which we felt should be avoided whenever possible.

8

Into Placement

A series of preplacement visits can achieve a great deal, provided it is used purposefully. Too often it is merely seen as a chance for child and family to get to know each other and ease the transition. Of course an easy transition is important, but we strove for more than this. We felt that, for both child and new parents, the whole introductory period provided an opportunity to make further progress in dealing with the unfinished business of coming to terms with past problems and increasing understanding and self-awareness. Families had to face the reality of an older child adoption – often very different from their original expectations. Some of them had to cope with a sudden upsurge of feelings about their infertility or the loss of a child which they thought they had already got over. Children had to come to a final acceptance that their future lay with a new family. Some could not make a final emotional break with their former family until they had a realistic hope of new parents. Others were still very frightened of making any emotional commitment. All had to transfer feelings of loyalty and affection from the St Luke's staff to their new family, and for some this was quite a painful process.

The timing of the actual placement was crucial. If it was too soon and the child unready, problems were inevitable. Too much delay could create equally severe difficulties. At this critical moment team-work was essential both as support and spur and we relied on each other a great deal.

We aimed for a smooth transference of the child's affections, loyalties and security. In reality every placement had its moments of doubt, its troughs and hillocks, its anxious consultations and minor or major adjustments of plan. One never knew when a hitch might occur. We found that we had to use all our knowledge of child development, our knowledge of this particular child and family, and our experiences of other placements. We also needed to keep our eyes and ears open and not make unfounded assumptions about what might be going on.

Philip provides a good example of an unexpected problem arising during introductions. The first few meetings between Philip, aged five, and Mr and Mrs Z. had gone well and he was due to visit them for a weekend. However, when Mr Z. arrived at St Luke's to collect him, Philip would have nothing to do with him and no amount of persuasion had any effect. So Brenda Murcer took Philip upstairs to his bedroom to try to find out what the problem was. At this point, the child started to cry and said that he didn't like Mr Z. Brenda tried to find out what it was he did not like, wondering whether it was his glasses, the way he spoke, etc. Eventually Philip felt able to ask why was it Mr Z. had so very little hair – he was almost bald. Brenda explained that some men do lose their hair, but it does not mean there is anything wrong with them, and then she talked to Philip about the familiar figures in his life who were bald or 'thinning'. Being thus reassured, Philip returned to a by now anxious Mr Z., climbed on his lap and started to feel his bald head with his fingers. Having satisfied himself that all was well, he was ready to leave for the weekend. When we explained to Mr Z. the problem that had arisen he accepted it easily and with considerable amusement. It was indeed an amusing incident, but if Brenda had not enabled Philip to explain his fears, but instead had relied upon a psychological interpretation of this little boy's behaviour, there would have been a real risk of misinterpretation and the whole placement might have been jeopardized.

With Susan, the anxious moment came right at the end of the introduction after a series of carefully planned visits. Susan was one of the first children to leave the Unit for a new family and we had not yet appreciated the problems that arose if prospective parents had to bring a child back to St Luke's after a visit. (Later we learned never to arrange things this way – see our comments in chapter 7.) When the time came for her new parents to go, Susan became tense and distressed and could not bring herself to say goodbye. It was suddenly obvious to

Brenda that the introductions were being too prolonged, and Susan no longer saw a return to St Luke's as security and respite from stress but felt that she was being left and perhaps rejected. The original plan for her to remain at St Luke's for another week, have a preplacement medical examination and pack her belongings at leisure had to be hastily rearranged. This four-year-old could not have tolerated such a delay. Permission for immediate placement – minus medical – had to be obtained from headquarters and the new mum came for her the very next day. Meanwhile Susan's house-mother had to do a lot of talking about moving to the new home for good and how nice it would be not to have to come back any more.

The minor set-back to Anthony's introduction caused by the Fs' having to postpone one visit has already been described. For the most part the rest of the introductions went quite smoothly, though there was one further occasion when he had a brief episode of fairly severe regression to the automaton-like state in which he had arrived at St Luke's. Because John Fitzgerald knew Anthony so well, he recognized what was happening and was able to help him over it quite quickly. The following brief excerpts from a detailed record of Anthony's placement show how things developed and the way in which this child followed a rather usual pattern in that he always left one of his own possessions at the foster home – to stake his claim, so to speak – and carried something of theirs back with him to St Luke's. In fact he carried Mr F.'s bottle-opener back and forth with him throughout the period of visits.

Foster parents' visit to Anthony at St Luke's
Anthony spent a relaxed and enjoyable afternoon with Mr and Mrs F. As arranged, I met with them towards the end of the afternoon to discuss progress thus far and the next step.

Both Mr and Mrs F. felt they were getting to know Anthony a little better. They commented that he still ignores them at first but today they asked him why and he apparently replied: 'Because you did not take me to your house.' However, the suggestion of going out for a walk soon brought him round. We arranged for Anthony to visit them the following Sunday for the day.

During the week following this visit Anthony had little to say about Mr and Mrs F. except that he was going to their house on Sunday. At one point when I was talking to him in the garden he got into a muddle over their name and finished up referring to them as 'Thems'. When I asked him if he found it hard to say their name he replied: 'Yes.' I suggested that, as the Fs call him by his first name, perhaps he would like to do the same and he said: 'Yes! What are their names?' I replied: 'Don and Gill.' He looked a little thoughtful but then looked up at me and said: 'Don and Gill', and grinned. I asked him if he knew which one was Don and which one was Gill and he replied: 'The man is Don and the lady Gill.' He grinned and then asked: 'Will you take me?' and I said I would. Then he said: 'On Sunday after pocket money.' I acknowledged that this was right and he went off to play in the sand-pit.

First visit to the prospective adopters

When I called to pick Anthony up at 8.00 a.m. he was ready and full of bounce. It was a very wet morning but he sat in the car very relaxed and interested in everything we saw on the journey. He stayed calm until the last 15 minutes, when he realized we were nearly there and became very excited. He started to jump up and down on the seat until he noticed my tool bag, then he quickly had my tools plus a tube of glue all over the front of the car.

When we arrived at the Fs' house Tony held on to my hand as we walked up the steps to the front door. However, once inside he started to run around exploring. This took quite a while, as it is a large bungalow. He suddenly burst into the lounge with Mr F. following and said: 'There's a bed', and ran out of the room. We all followed to see what he was referring to and found him in a small bedroom bouncing up and down on a small single bed saying repeatedly: 'My bed! My bed!' He then raced out of the room again to continue his exploration. After a few minutes he returned to the lounge and started to look at the small ornaments around the room. Suddenly he began to pick them up one by one saying: 'Mine.' Once he had as many as he could carry he took them to the small bedroom and deposited them on the table beside the bed.

... When I joined them in the garden I suggested to Anthony that I might be leaving for a short while but he became very clinging and said: 'I don't want you to go.' I therefore assured him I would not leave him and Mr and Mrs F. were quite agreeable for me to stay.

I tried to keep in the background as much as possible to allow Tony and Mr and Mrs F. to spend as much time together as possible. Tony spent most of the time up to lunch 'helping' Mrs F. in the kitchen. By this stage he had calmed down and was behaving in a very normal way. He was relaxed and enjoyed his lunch.

In the afternoon, we visited Mr and Mrs F.'s shop at Tony's

request. Back at the house Anthony insisted on leaving his packet of jelly babies (which he had purchased at a motorway service centre on the way) in Mr F.'s car.

Through tea, he was relaxed and sensible but afterwards started to show some anxiety at the suggestion of leaving. I asked him if he would like to visit Mr and Mrs F. again and he grinned, said 'Yes!' and then relaxed. However, when he came to leave he picked up Mr F.'s bottle-opener and insisted on bringing it with him, saying: 'I bring it Sunday.'

During the week following this visit Anthony was very excitable and very boisterous in a way which led him into conflict with others in the house. However, he was unable to say why he was behaving in this way but asked me on a number of occasions: 'When is Sunday?' and then he would work out that it was the day after he got his pocket money and he would grin with pleasure.

Second visit to the prospective adopters

Anthony was again very bright and full of bounce, and came out to the car holding Mr F.'s bottle-opener. He showed no signs of anxiety on the journey, and indeed when we arrived could not wait for me to lock the car before running up the steps to ring the door bell. He greeted Mrs F. with a kiss and a hug before marching into the house and taking his coat off. He placed Mr F.'s bottle-opener on the hall table and went off to look round the house to make sure everything was as it was last week. After we had been in the house for a few minutes Mr F. arrived home (he had been to the shop) and Tony greeted him with obvious pleasure. Tony showed him the bottle-opener and then asked for the jelly babies. They both went off to the car to find them. When they returned, I suggested to Tony that I would not be staying but would come back after tea to collect him. He just shrugged his shoulders, said 'Yes!' and went off to the garden with Mr F.

... During the course of the day he asked Mr and Mrs F.: 'Are you my new Mummy and Daddy?' They apparently evaded this by saying: 'Why do you think that?' Anthony said: 'I know', and then decided to go off to water the garden.

Third visit

After getting out of the car outside the Fs' house Tony lay down on the grass and buried his face in his hands. It was a couple of minutes before he recovered his composure and bounded up the steps to Mr and Mrs F. Once inside the house he was not the least bit interested in me and I was able to leave him after a few minutes.

When I returned a few hours later I learned that the morning had gone well, but after lunch Tony had become very quiet and impassive, and though obedient had lost his usual bounce and had to be told what to do all the time. He reminded me of the old Anthony of his early days at St Luke's, when he had been totally stiff and unresponsive and stayed wherever he was put.

It occurred to me that he was probably comparing this with his previous foster home and perhaps feared things would be the same. It seemed best to try and bring this out into the open, so I suggested to Tony that we go along to 'his' room and have a chat. He followed me obediently.

After a few general remarks, I said: 'Mrs F. isn't a bit like Mrs D., is she?' 'No', he replied. 'Can you tell me how she's different?' 'Well, she's fatter', he said, 'and older. Her voice is different. She cuddles me a lot.' Then he laughed and said:, 'And the food's much better.' This seemed to release his tension and he was over the withdrawn phase again. Just what triggered it, we did not know.

... When I arrived at St Luke's next morning I found Anthony sitting ouside the playroom door. The play leader told me that he had become more and more excitable during the course of the morning until he got to the point when his behaviour was bordering on recklessness. For his own safety she had to put him outside the door so as to give him an opportunity to calm down. When she asked him why he was behaving so recklessly he could not tell her. He had evidently swung back to the opposite extreme of the zombie-like behaviour of the previous afternoon.

After lunch, Anthony went quite happily to the front sitting-room with me – indeed he demanded to do so. We talked about his behaviour that morning but he could not tell me why he had got so excited. His 'I don't know' was accompanied by a look of frustration. He suddenly said:, 'When we go there again?' I asked if he meant to the Fs' house and he replied: 'Yes.' However, before I could comment, Tony said: 'We go next Sunday.' I asked him if he wanted to go just for the day again. He replied: 'Yes!' and then added: 'I want to stay one day.' I asked him if he meant he wanted to sleep there and he said: 'Think so', and added: 'All Sundays.' He was looking a bit perplexed but brightened up to say: 'I could stay there.' I asked if he thought the bed would be nice to sleep in and he replied hesitatingly: 'Yes, but if it is crunchy I will only stay Sundays.' I then suggested that perhaps our next visit should be just for the day, and then we could discuss with Mr and Mrs F. whether he could go to stay for one night the following weekend. He grinned and said: 'Yes', and went happily to the garden.

Fourth visit

... When I returned to collect Tony, Mr F. told me that at one point during the afternoon Anthony had decided to sit on the bed in the spare room and he asked Mrs F. to read him a story whilst he snuggled down under the bedspread. However, he had not mentioned wanting to sleep at their house and so I had a talk with him. I first asked him if he remembered what we had talked about the previous Monday and he said he did. I then asked if he was going to ask Mr and Mrs F. the question that he wanted to put to them, and he shook his head and buried his face in his hands once again. When I asked him if he would like me to pretend to be him and ask the question for him he relaxed, beamed all over his face and said: 'Yes, please.' So I pretended to be Tony and asked Mrs F. if I could stay overnight for one night and of course she agreed, at which Tony seemed very pleased.

When it was time for us to leave, he checked with Mr F. that his packet of jelly babies was still in the car and once again insisted on taking the bottle-opener home with him.

(After several overnight visits Anthony spent the weekend with the F s.)

On arrival at the Fs' home to collect Tony he seemed to be fairly relaxed, but I learnt from Mrs F. that, following my phone call on the previous day, he had been somewhat chaotic in his behaviour and they had great difficulty in exerting any control. From their description it seemed to be very similar to the kind of behaviour we have experienced at Balham when Anthony has been suffering from anxiety on a particular point. As it apparently commenced after my telephone call, it may well be that Anthony is identifying much more with the F s now and my call may have been an unwelcome reminder that he had to return to St Luke's. It was fairly obvious that he was not quite ready to leave the F s' home with me and there are signs that he is increasingly identifying with this family.

On the way home, Tony said: 'Why does time go so fast?' I suggested that when you are doing something you like time appears to go more quickly than when you are doing something you don't like. He looked rather thoughtful and then said: 'The time went too fast.' I asked him if he thought this could be because he liked coming to see Mr and Mrs F. and he said: 'Yes, but can I come next time for a big time?' I said that I would obviously have to have a word with Mr and Mrs F. and his house-parents, and this seemed to please him.

In the week following this visit Tony found another way to show us how he felt about his new family. He took to 'swimming' in the bath and when asked where he was going invariably named the town in which the Fs lived. We felt confident that this was the right placement for Tony but, because this was a child who had been too passive in the past, we felt it was particularly important that he now make a definite decision for himself and be able to articulate it even if this meant prolonging the visiting period a little more.

This final step was achieved when Tony went to the Fs' for a week's visit. On this occasion Brenda took him on the train and during the journey Tony suddenly said: 'I want to stay and be their little boy.' 'For ever and ever?' questioned Brenda. 'Yes.' 'So when you live there, will you come back and visit St Luke's?' 'No', he replied, 'because it wouldn't be my home then.' Tony had clearly been thinking things out quite carefully.

John's report after this final introductory visit also reflects Tony's increased confidence and the way he had sorted things out in his mind and become able to express his feelings. It was three months since the Fs' first visit and the placement was the fruit of a great deal of hard work by everyone concerned – not least Tony and his new parents.

Final preplacement visit

I visited during Anthony's holiday. Mrs F. told me that things had gone smoothly and that they were just waiting for the time when Anthony went to live with them permanently. After a short time Tony appeared and asked me to go and see the model aeroplane that he was making. Even before we reached his room he said: 'Am I coming with you the day after tomorrow to St Luke's?' I said yes, and asked him how he felt about this. He replied: 'If I go with you I'm not staying long. I'm coming back to Mummy Gill and Daddy Don.' I explored this a little further with him and it was obvious that his future is with the Fs and that in his own way he has worked out the implications of the move from Balham.

Satisified by my comment that I would ask his house-parents about it when I returned, we continued on our way to see the aeroplane. It was quite an interesting model in that he was using a real hammer and nails and had nailed several pieces of wood together so that no-one could fail to see what it was meant to be. He was obviously very proud of this but said: 'I want one more nail in here', pointing to a spot in the middle of the model. He then asked me: 'Will you do it?' When I asked why he replied: 'Well, it takes me so long that my hand gets tired, and any case I will mark it so that you know it is your nail'. This appears to be Tony's way of taking just a little bit of his previous environment into his new family.

As we built up our experience of placing children in families, we learned that all of them had phases when they appeared to be anxious, miserable or withdrawn. These varied in timing and intensity with each child but there were periods in virtually every case when, if we had interpreted their behaviour in a simplistic manner, we might have concluded either that the child would never be able to relate to the particular family or that he or she was unplaceable.

When one is confronted with an apparently unhappy or withdrawn child, it is easy to assume quite mistakenly that the cause is directly related to a current experience in a negative way. The sensitive network of communication between the St Luke's staff and children proved invaluable in this regard and often prevented inappropriate decisions being made. We came to realize that, during the introductory process, difficult phases of the child's behaviour were likely to occur when he was wrestling with his feelings about the past, present and future. Positive help to sort out these feelings, far from ending the relationship with the substitute family, served to strengthen it. The difficult behaviour served as an indication that the child had inner conflict and needed help. Through observing the behaviour, through entering into the child's play, through providing opportunities to talk, through pooling the united knowledge, observation and understanding of the team, we sought to uncover the source of the problem and help the child to deal with it.

This sounds rather complicated and difficult. In fact the direct help was often very simple in itself – perhaps just a few words which accepted a child's feelings of anger against a natural parent as reasonable and right or a comment about his new family which showed that we did not consider him disloyal if he wanted to leave us and go to live with them. The difficult thing is to create the atmosphere of understanding and teamwork that makes it possible to offer this simple but essential help to a child in taking a decisive step forward.

We have emphasized all the way through the need for every member of staff to be sensitive to the child's needs, feelings and views. When the youngster is wrestling with the final decision over moving to a new family this is particularly relevant. We found that children needed a great deal of support before they could communicate a wish to leave St Luke's, partly because of the implications of committing themselves to a new way of life, but also because they had feelings about not rejecting us – the latter point being one we feel should not be underestimated. Because of this we sometimes found that a child might say he wished to live with a particular family, but at the same time make an objection to it happening.

Selecting the right moment to offer help is a perennial problem. If a child who is wrestling with a decision is just left to sort out his anxieties for himself, one can miss the optimum moment altogether. However, if one moves in too quickly with support it can be perceived by the child as pressure. No child should be placed while in a state of inner conflict. But if the conflict is over the actual move, it may be vital to proceed rapidly once the problem comes to the surface and is resolved. Testing it out with further visits could throw the whole situation back to square one. We found it an essential precaution that in discussions with child or couple no member of the team would commit us to a course of action without consulting the other team members. A well-used question was: Shall we talk to Bill and Brenda Murcer or to John Fitzgerald or 'whoever' about it?

Without the support of the other members of the team there would have been many occasions when one or other of us might well have made an inappropriate decision either to break off or to rush a placement. Every placement creates considerable anxiety, and staff members have a high investment in the outcome. This can influence professional judgement, and the greater objectivity of the rest of the team is an important balance. The final stages of Philip's placement offer an example of useful teamwork.

Philip had been acting-out within the school setting for about two weeks and exhibiting increasing aggression towards the teacher. We were aware that we were near to the point when Philip would have to make a decision, but we hesitated to create an opportunity for him to put his feelings into words because we were frankly perplexed by his behaviour. The cause of our confusion was that Philip was being aggressive towards his *female* teacher, and the prospective substitute mother, Mrs Z., was also a teacher. We were trying to work out the significance of these two facts and were puzzled because the only interpretive conclusion we could come to was that although Philip seemed to enjoy his contacts with the Zs, he must want to end the relationship and be projecting his feelings about Mrs Z. on to his teacher. Not only was this interpretation wrong, our hesitation almost caused us to miss the optimum moment to discover Philip's true feelings. Fortunately, at a staff conference, we decided to put our interpretive conclusions on one side whilst Bill Murcer talked with Philip. Although Bill attempted this, Philip's anxiety level was so high that he could not discuss his feelings. Aware that we were running out of time, we decided that it might be worth trying to reach Philip in a neutral setting away from St Luke's. So John Fitzgerald took him to a local park, where they walked around the lake which had on it a number of ducks and their offspring.

Philip relaxed almost as soon as he left the Unit. He noticed the ducks and immediately started to ask John about the home life of mother ducks, father ducks and baby ducks. 'Where do they live? Are they happy? If the ducks lived in a children's home, would they want a new Mummy and Daddy like Mr and Mrs Z.?' John Fitzgerald answered the first two questions, but turned the third back to Philip and asked if he thought they would like a new Mummy and Daddy like Mr and Mrs Z. 'No', Philip replied. 'Why?' 'Because I want to live there and there won't be room for us all.' At the suggestion that John should ask Bill and Brenda Murcer and Mr and Mrs Z. if he could go to live with the Zs for good, Philip was very excited and insisted on returning to St Luke's to arrange matters immediately! We had misread the clues and nearly missed the boat. Philip's anxiety made it impossible for him to work through to the decision which he really wanted to make, and the whole incident served to remind us once again of the need to be responsive to children and not rely simply on our powers of observation or interpretation.

So far in this chapter it may have seemed that the hesitations and need for help were all in relation to the child. In reality, of course, problems could and did arise in regard to the prospective parents or with members of staff. It occasionally happened that a staff member would feel hurt by a child's eagerness to leave and would begin to reject the child as a way of minimizing her own pain. In such a situation it was important for senior staff to offer a lot of support and try to help people understand what was going on.

Whereas for residential staff help was always at hand, the new family were mostly on their own. There were times when local social workers needed to move in quickly with inter-pretations, explanations or just reassurance. Such an occasion arose shortly before Anthony went to live with Mr and Mrs F. Although the introductions were going very well, the Fs were suddenly taken with an attack of anxiety about what Anthony would be losing when he came to them for good. They knew he loved the people at St Luke's and they could see that he was a boy who enjoyed the company of other children. They were childless. They felt guilty about asking him to leave Balham and feared he might not be happy with them. It was difficult for them to express these feelings to staff at St Luke's.

Fortunately they had a good relationship with their local social worker. She visited quickly and helped them to remember all the benefits that Tony would enjoy when he had parents and a home of his own. She also pointed out that all decisions in life involve some loss, and moving into a new family is no exception. With their momentary panic recognized and accepted and their fears assuaged, the Fs were able to go forward again with confidence but, without the social worker's help, their doubts might well have been picked up by Tony and a downward spiral of anxiety set in.

Although the family's main support came from their own social worker, they required from the team reassurance of progress, reassurance that they were handling situations correctly and alleviation of specific anxiety. We mentioned earlier that during this period one aspect of the child's process of familiarization is the comparison of the new situation with past experiences. This can be difficult for the prospective parents. Tim provides a good illustration of how a child can heighten a family's anxiety level.

During one of his visits to the Ms' home they showed him a small plaque to be fixed to the door of what was to be his room. It had the words 'Tim's Room' on it. His reaction was to say very simply: 'I had one of those in my last house', and change the subject. Mr and Mrs M. had, of course, expected a pleasurable reaction. They were not only deflated by Timothy's response, it left them feeling very anxious. It was necessary for the team to discuss the incident with them very fully. We reminded them of our earlier discussions, when we had pointed out that Tim would inevitably compare their home with his past experience and explained that far from rejecting them, as Mr and Mrs M. feared, the boy could simply be making a straight comparison. We went on to remind the Ms of earlier discussions when we had emphasized the need to move at the child's pace. We gently pointed out that, in offering the plaque to Tim, they were asking him to accept that he was going to live with them – a decision that he was not yet emotionally ready to make. Mr and Mrs M. readily saw the implication and felt rather guilty about what they saw as making a mistake. However, they were able to draw on the memory of the earlier discussions and accept our reassurance that many substitute families make this sort of error of judgement simply because of their enthusiasm, and it need not be serious or cause any long-lasting ill effect.

The interesting thing is that, when situations like this arose, almost without exception the families were able to recall comments we had made at the early preparatory discussions and which they could now relate to the specific problem with which we were dealing. Although they might have to be reminded of those early discussions, they were able to see that the kind of predictions we had made in a general sense were now happening in specific ways. This had the effect of strengthening the relationship between the substitute family and the agency in a way which would eventually make the post-placement supervision a positive and constructive experience for everyone.

Sometimes the problems which arose with prospective parents were much more serious than the little incident over the wall plaque. Just after John Fitzgerald left St Luke's to become an area manager, the Unit went through a very difficult placement which was written up in great detail by one of the residential staff. The problem was the prospective parents' eight-year-old son, their apparent inability to control him and our doubts about whether he could adjust to a younger sister and whether the parents could cope with two difficult children. The child we were hoping to place was six-year-old Sheila who, as readers may remember from previous chapters, was a small but strong-willed little person capable of manipulative behaviour and afraid of close relationships.

The various problems had to be overcome before the new family and the St Luke's team could feel confident that the placement should go ahead. There were times when people despaired of a successful outcome and a great deal of work was required. Team support for both staff and family was essential.

The new family consisted of Jane and Gilbert Y. and their son Donald, aged eight. The local social worker, Mrs W., knew them well and had confidence in them, but there were times during the introduction when the St Luke's staff were full of doubts about whether the Ys could cope with Sheila as well as Donald. Both children could display quite difficult behaviour and the Ys were not always able to control Donald very well.

From the Ys' point of view, the first two meetings went badly. It had been decided that the Ys should come to St. Luke's and meet Sheila on a casual basis, and would not at first be introduced as possible new parents. Jane Y. was very anxious beforehand and, as she herself put it, had worked herself up into such a state about seeing Sheila that she could not take in anything at all when she reached Balham. She was completely overwhelmed. It was therefore agreed that the Ys should come for another 'first visit'. This was not much better. Mr and Mrs Y. tried to push Donald into a relationship with Sheila and he responded by acting up. The detailed record of the meeting says that he 'chased Sheila around the table, fought with one boy, teased another and began hitting his parents with some degree of aggression'.

Later, when Donald had gone out to play on the climbing

frame and Sheila was back in the classroom, Jane and Gilbert had a chance to talk with two members of staff. Jane apologized for not having said much the previous week, but said that she had been so overcome she had been struck dumb. Her main worry, she said, was that she had not felt she loved Sheila. She said that she realized now that she had been waiting so long she had built up a completely idealized picture, and had found instead an ordinary little girl. She had expected to feel a rush of affection but had thought instead: 'Oh, so this is Sheila.' She felt 'unnatural' and also felt a considerable degree of responsibility towards Sheila.

The St Luke's staff felt that Jane was a very compassionate person who wanted to be sure that she could love Sheila and was frightened of hurting her. The record goes on:

We were concerned about the visit at the time. The more we thought about it the more worried we became. Mrs Y. seemed likely to worry herself into the ground and there was the anxiety on our part that she might go ahead with the introduction, feeling doubts but thinking: 'Well, we've got this far. Perhaps it will be all right', then think, upon the occasion of a breakdown: 'Well I never did take to the child.'

Our main worry, however, was Donald. He was completely unable to cope with the situation and we were left wondering how much we could expect from any child of eight. As for his acting-out behaviour, we did not know how much of it we should excuse because of the situation, or how much the lack of control on the part of the parents was the norm. And if he was behaving in such an unruly manner because he was overwhelmed, what then was the situation doing to him?

In spite of these initial set-backs, Mrs W., the social worker, remained confident that the Y. family had a lot to offer so, rather sceptically, the St Luke's team agreed to another visit. It was a success. The Ys had evidently done a lot of thinking and talking with each other and with Mrs W. They were still keen to get to know Sheila and she, in turn, responded favourably to them. Two more day visits were arranged and Sheila was helped to understand that the Ys hoped to have another child as a member of their family. She continued to react positively and when the Ys spent a weekend at St Luke's further progress was made. However, there were still some doubts about Donald's relationship with his parents and whether Jane and Gilbert would be able to cope if both Donald and Sheila 'played up' at the same time. One of the residential staff commented:

We feel very happy with Jane and Gilbert now. They are both still worrity and nervous, but show perception and sense with regard to Sheila. But we do have nagging doubts about Donald. Personally, I hover between irritation and astonishment at how well he is coping. I think that it is easy, with Donald, to take for granted some of the very difficult experiences with which he is coping well and see only those elements of his character which are worrying, because one expects to be worried by the 'other child' in a fostering introduction.

The next set-back was that, when the Ys came for a second weekend, Sheila 'took fright' and refused to go out with Jane and Gilbert. This reaction was not unexpected and the Ys had been warned that it might happen. They were distressed but showed understanding, and it helped them realize how much they already minded about Sheila. Although Sheila 'played hot and cold' all weekend and upset and confused poor Donald, one big hurdle was overcome at bathtime. When Jane said to Sheila: 'Come on, it's time to get out of the bath now', Sheila looked her in the eye and said: 'Make me.' Jane took prompt action and did not need to be told that this was a good sign, though she did need a lot of reassurance about how things might go when Sheila came to them for her first visit.

At the end of this rather difficult weekend there was a feeling of relief at St Luke's that Sheila was becoming emotionally involved and not just 'floating through' the introduction in a superficial way. But some doubts remained:

I think that Sheila is becoming genuinely attached to all three Ys. They are her kind of people – fairly simple but perceptive, relaxed, not very demanding, warm. Really nice people, in fact. I hope that Sheila goes to live with them, but we all feel that at the moment something, somewhere, is not quite right.

During Sheila's subsequent visits to the Ys' home, it became clear that the central issue was their ability to control Donald. The St Luke's staff and Mrs W. were hesitant to interfere with these parents' methods of handling their child, yet they feared that Sheila would never have confidence in Jane and Gilbert's ability to control *her*, if she could not see them cope with Donald. A plan was evolved for the Y. family to join in a camping holiday with a group from St Luke's. Sheila immediately chose to change her tent and share with Donald Y. The record gives a detailed account of developments:

The first couple of days at camp were extremely difficult on the Donald front. His behaviour at this point was not abominable, as it was during Sheila's visits to the foster home, but it still showed very distinct signs of sulkiness and manipulation – the same old story of always having the last word. Sheila wasn't playing them up but was quietly watching Donald. It was obvious that soon she was either going to decide quietly and irrevocably that it was a bad situation, in which case we would have supported her, or she was going to start playing up herself, in which case the situation was going to come to a crisis.

We had agreed with Mrs W. before camp that Jane and Gilbert had got to work out for themselves that they couldn't allow two children to get away with what they had got into the habit of allowing an only child to get away with, particularly since the two youngsters were very similar in temperament. Jane Y. was either going to end up with a very sound relationship with Sheila and a better relationship with Donald, or else a poor relationship with both and a bad state of nerves. We felt that Jane probably did have the insight, the reserves and the relationship with Donald to weather the storm, but we felt that we couldn't risk letting Sheila go to live with them until it began to be obvious which way it was going to go.

On about the third morning, Gilbert remarked that Sheila was watching very closely to see how far Donald could go, and was obviously going to follow suit. We were very pleased that it was Gilbert who said this, because this provided the opportunity to talk about how Sheila would follow Donald and how she wouldn't feel safe till she knew where she stood and Donald knew where he stood. I talked, particularly to Jane, about the sort of tricks Sheila can pull, how manipulating she can be, how convincing she can be when she puts her face in her hands and sulks and puts on a 'performance'. I never once mentioned Donald but Jane took the point.

Sheila gradually disassociated herself from the rest of us. It soon became 'our tent' and 'our car'. Superficially there was a family of four who were all close friends of ours camping with us, that was all.

In fact, they were all very much more reliant on us than that, but that was the appearance they gave.

There was a very tricky couple of days when Sheila and Donald played up one after the other. When one stopped, the other started. Moan, wail, complain, shout. It was just as we had predicted it could be and both children together were enough to drive anyone mad. Had I been Jane I think I'd have banged their heads together. It was very hard to stand worriedly on the sidelines, sweating it out, offering advice when it was asked for and giving really fairly intensive support but without direct comment.

Finally, on the Tuesday evening, Sheila had a showdown with Jane. We learned that Sheila had insisted upon taking a plastic windmill to bed with her. Jane said 'No' and Sheila had ranted and raved and cried and called her all the names under the sun. Jane had come out of the tent toward the end, but Gilbert had sent her back to finish it off. She held her ground and won the battle but was terribly afraid that Sheila would never speak to her again and was desperately worried about why it had happened. When I heard this I said: 'She was having you on – she'll be as right as rain by now! That's Sheila. She'll try it on but there's no hard feelings when she's beaten.' Gilbert burst out laughing. Jane looked supremely doubtful, but went to the tent and was overcome with relief to find out that I was right. Donald had sat in stunned silence during the entire performance, venturing only a subdued 'Goodnight' when Jane finally flounced out of the tent. I think it was a case of 'To see ourselves as others see us.'

We talked for ages about how difficult it is to let fly at a child when you're trying to build up a relationship. I repeated many times that it is necessary not to let Sheila hoodwink you and emphasized how firm one must be with her. Jane and Gilbert would never be too harsh with her, so it was quite safe to say that.

Gilbert learnt the knack the following day of not getting involved in a 'who exactly did what' dispute but employed the 'Right, *both* of you sit down and behave' tactics. Gradually signs of improvement began to appear. Donald always has taken notice of his father and seemed very much happier now that Gilbert was exerting his authority over both him and Sheila. At this point the Ys made the difficult but imperceptible shift from having one child and 'half a child, half a visitor' to having two children who were both treated equally. I think, in retrospect, that this perhaps made things easier for Donald. Certainly there was a much better 'feel' to him, though he still played up to a certain extent. I think it was very good for him to be with Sheila and his parents twenty-four hours a day, but not in his own home and not at St Luke's.

Sheila was so much one of the family that I suggested to her that she might like to travel to their home on the Saturday and I would come and collect her on the Tuesday. I didn't know how she would take it and expected her to change her mind. She went without the slightest hesitation. I gave her my torch and told her to be sure to give me it back on Tuesday, but she didn't really need it or want it. I think she only took it to humour me.

From this time onwards the road was virtually downhill all the way to Sheila's final and successful placement with the Ys, but the very real anxiety that is displayed in the foregoing report highlights the investment residential staff are bound to have in achieving a successful fostering or adoptive placement. It can be difficult for staff who have worked so hard and so closely with the child to 'let go' and free him to move on to his new family. Inevitably there is some feeling of rejection as the child on whom so much affection and effort has been expended makes the deliberate – and appropriate – choice to leave and join a new family. At St Luke's the child's 'special person' was of course most at risk in this respect. Other members of staff needed to be alert to the need to offer support, while the person most concerned had to be open to her own feelings and aware of her reactions, so as to be sure not to reject the child in response to his increasing attachment to substitute parents and loosening of ties with St Luke's.

Projection of staff anxieties or other feelings on to either child or family can easily wreck a placement. The use of the group, the involvement of our psychiatric adviser and a watchful eye by senior members of staff on each other and on junior colleagues were all necessary and much used safeguards. We tried to ensure that all doubts and worries were brought out into the open, having learned to our cost that, if anyone smothered his or her doubts, crucial clues might be overlooked and inappropriate plans be set in motion or continued. The early and continued involvement of staff in selection of families, the passing on of information and preparation and the support of families and children throughout the intro- duction made the whole process of weaning positive and gradual and helped to prevent possessiveness.

When planning introductions, it was important to consider

timing in relation to the child's special person. We felt it was important that, when a real bond had been formed, the child should have the security of knowing that his 'special person' knew and liked his new family and that she approved the plan for placement. Sometimes this created real dilemmas. For instance, just at the moment when Jean, who was Valerie's very special person, was about to go to America for several months, a new family was suggested for Valerie. Our anxiety was that if we began the introductions just when Jean was leaving, Valerie's feelings of loss might complicate her approach to new parents. On the other hand, if we postponed the introductions until Jean had gone, Valerie might feel disloyal to Jean in transferring her affections and become even more emotionally confused. After a great deal of thought and discussion, it was decided that the most important thing in the long term was to assure Valerie that Jean knew and approved her prospective family. This would then make it possible for other staff members to talk to Valerie about the fact that Jean knew and liked them and, if necessary, assure her that Jean would be happy if she found a family. We knew that we were putting quite an emotional load on this child in expecting her to cope with Jean's departure and meeting new parents within a short space of time, but it seemed the 'lesser evil'. In the event, our decision seemed right. The introductions went reasonably smoothly, even though the first meetings were slightly complicated by the need to have Jean's involvement with the prospective parents clearly demonstrated. Fortunately Jean was mature in outlook, even though still young in years; she was also conscientious in keeping in touch with Valerie during her trip, and tapered off her involvement in a very sensitive and appropriate way.

9

Afterwards

Central to the planning for placement was the knowledge that, when the child moved, a new family was being created, and each member of the new family would have needs which the social work staff attempted to meet. The child was leaving behind an important period of his life and the people involved, but to sever the contact would have been damaging, although in time he would make that choice himself. The family were conscious that they were inheriting the child's exisiting attachments and establishing new ones. *All* the children were moving into new families where legal adoption was the intended status of the placement.

With these factors in mind, the post-placement work was carried out jointly by the family's own social worker and staff of the Long-Stay Unit. To avoid confusion and conflict, a clear role was devised for those working with the child and his new parents, agreed objectives set and a programme and method of work designed.

If one starts from a perspective that both the child and the adults in the new family have needs, defining a role for the staff involved becomes fairly straightforward, and this also determines which staff should participate.

Once the child moved into placement, either John, as the Unit's social worker, or the child's special house-mother would visit the home as well as the family's own social worker. The Unit's staff were clear that their role was to form the bridge from the child's past to the future. The family social worker's task was to be available to help the new parents to adjust to the changes that were taking place. Both social workers would seek to interpret the child's behaviour and reactions. The key to ensuring that the respective roles did not confuse or conflict was good communciation.

The overall objective of post-placement work was, of course, to enable the new parents to take over full responsibility for the care of the child and integrate him into their family structure. However, before this goal could be achieved there were other objectives to be accomplished. First, the child had to separate emotionally from the Long-Stay Unit so that he could make a full attachment to his new family. Second, the family had to develop the confidence to cope with and understand the child's needs so that they, in turn, could attach to him.

A visiting programme was designed for the first month which ensured that a visit to the new family was made during the first week of the placement and weekly thereafter. The first visit was always made jointly by the family's social worker and the designated member of the Unit's staff. We felt that this early visit was important, both to reassure the child that his past still existed and to enable the family to explore uncertainties about the way they were handling day to day situations. The plan was always discussed fully with the child and family before placement.

The following extract from the case record of Philip and Mr and Mrs Z., whom the reader met in earlier chapters, illustrates what we mean. When John and the area social worker arrived at the house they found the whole family at home:

At first Philip stayed very close to Mrs Z, saying little. However, after about ten minutes he started to move very slowly away from Mrs Z., and inch his way around the room. At first it looked as though he were heading towards some sweets on the sideboard, but he passed them by and continued until he reached the chair John was sitting on. Philip sat down on the floor leaning against John's leg but still did not join in the conversation and avoided John's attempts to engage him. After another ten minutes, Philip moved away from John and edged his way back around the room to Mr Z. Suddenly, very brightly, he said to Mr Z.: 'Can we make some tea?' Mr Z. quickly agreed and Philip went with him to the kitchen. Whilst the tea was being made Mrs Z. told us that the only problem they had had was a wet bed the second night. She recalled that this was something we had warned might happen, given Philip's previous pattern when anxious. Mrs Z.

went on to describe how they had dealt with Philip very gently and had not made an issue of it with Philip. She then sought our assurance that they had handled the problem properly.

During those first visits we would not attempt to split the family and child for separate contact, but we found that there were always plenty of natural breaks to enable discussion with either the child or the family individually. Anthony, for example, insisted on taking John to see his bedroom and the new bedroom furniture. Once there, he told John how he had been allowed to go to Mr and Mrs F.'s shop and the fun he had had playing at shopkeepers. He still had a need to share his excitement with those from his immediate past.

For the remainder of the first month alternate joint visits would be made, with the family's social worker visiting in between. This pattern would be understood by both child and family, but it was crucial that each visit should be fully recorded, with copies of the reports going to all who were involved, plus discussion between the social workers. Anxiety levels are higher at this delicate state and frequent visiting ensured that early difficulties did not become major problems.

Again Philip illustrates this point. At the end of three weeks the family's social worker visited again, on her own, and found Philip apparently lively and enjoying life, whilst Mr and Mrs Z. were looking jaded. It transpired that during the day Philip appeared very secure and yet he was now wetting his bed every night. The social worker explored with Mrs Z. the various potential causes, trying to isolate the possible anxiety at the root of the problem, but neither of them felt that they had got to the bottom of it. It was agreed that the social worker would discuss the problem with the St Luke's staff. When that discussion took place, everyone was conscious of the way Philip had presented problems in the past and how he had a habit of confusing us. We tried to look for alternative explanations for the bed-wetting, other than just anxiety about being with his new family. Bill and Brenda recalled a long period just after his arrival at St Luke's when Philip had wet his bed. During that period there was no doubt he was anxious about the trauma in his life, but it was a fear of moving out of his bed to visit the toilet in strange surroundings which resulted in the wet beds. They had solved the problem by waking him each night just before they went to bed and taking him to the toilet. After a few weeks he got used to getting up and felt secure enough to visit the toilet on his own, until his anxiety level subsided and with it his need to visit the toilet during the night.

The family's social worker telephoned Mrs Z. and explained what had happened previously at St Luke's and suggested they tried the same approach. When she visited with John a week later there had been no further wet beds, and over the next three months the need to get up in the night disappeared too.

The frequency of visits after the first month was determined by the individual circumstances of each placement, as was the degree of involvement by the Unit's staff. Visits by the Unit's staff were usually made jointly with the family's social worker. Occasionally John would visit on his own, but we learned to be very cautious about doing that after inadvertently creating unnecessary stress for a particular child. This was a boy called Leonard who had been in placement three months, and John was due to make a joint visit with the family's social worker. Unfortunately at the last minute the social worker was unable to come and left John to go on his own. As soon as John had entered the house Leonard became very distressed. After some minutes it transpired that the lad thought that, because John had called on his own, he had come to take him back to St Luke's. It took considerable persuasion to convince him otherwise. After that incident, we were careful to ensure that the child, if being visited by one of our staff alone, understood that it was just a visit.

During these early months some children would ask to return to St Luke's for a visit, just to reassure themselves that the past they remembered was real, whilst others showed no desire to return. This could be a difficult area for families. Conscientiously they would want to ensure that links with the past were not inappropriately broken, and consequently many children came back for a pleasurable reunion. However, we were reminded yet again of how important it is to look at an individual child's needs and not just to follow rigid rules. Anthony's family tried to ensure that the positive links from his past were not forgotten, but found that when they visited St

Luke's he became very upset. He had transferred his attachments to his new family and the return visit threatened his new-found security.

After the child had been in placement for three months, a review conference was held at St Luke's. The participants included the family's social worker and her area officer, the consultant psychiatrist, educational psychologist, teacher, St Luke's residential staff and field social worker. Looking back now, we feel that in some cases we could have enhanced the discussions and decision making had we included the new family. The tasks of the conference were:

1   to review the progress of the placement to date,
2   to explore any particular problems that were being presented and decide how they should be dealt with,
3   to determine the degree of future involvement of the Unit's staff in the placement, and
4   to agree the timing of the full transfer of responsibility for the placement to the Children's Society's area team in the family's home area.

The latter decision was important because so many of the children were placed over very long distances, anything between 100 and 400 miles, and, whilst we in the Unit could offer some support over the short term, it was not possible for us to provide intensive work over a longer term.

Those who have been involved in inter-agency work will know how important trust is to this kind of decision. We were fortunate that all the social workers whose families we used shared a very positive relationship with us. Having built a close working relationship through the process of introduction and placement, we were able to hand over responsibility to colleagues we could trust and respect. Although overall responsibility passed to a different group of social work staff, we would retain some contact with each child until the moment arrived when it was clear he no longer needed us.

As with all the work with children at St Luke's, the moment for final withdrawal of the Unit's staff was determined by the needs of the child and his own wishes. When John visited children in their new families, he looked for evidence that the child's new attachments had replaced those from St Luke's.

Children could and did communicate their views on this in a variety of ways. Anthony, for example, now aged seven, simply told John that he 'did not have to come any more because I live with Mr and Mrs F. now'. Philip, on the other hand, conveyed his views in his usual indirect way. John went to see him after he had been living with Mr and Mrs Z. for six months, but when he arrived there was no sign of Philip. Mrs Z. said that Philip was a few gardens away playing football with some new-found friends, and after about twenty minutes Mr Z. went to collect him. However, when Philip arrived, he simply said: 'Hello, John, goodbye', went straight out of the house and back to his friends. He had decided to 'vote with his feet'.

When we knew that we were probably seeing for the last time a child with whom we had been through so much, it was natural to feel a twinge of sadness. However, these feelings were more than compensated for by the knowledge that the child was settled and happy with his new family.

10

Reflections

In describing our methods of work, we are conscious that we have presented our own perspectives. How did the 'consumer' perceive what we were attempting to do? To round out the picture a little, we asked a former St Luke's child and his adoptive family to reflect back on their experiences of working with us. Their comments, which follow, are taken directly from a taped discussion. Martin was seven when he first met Mr and Mrs C. He had lived at St Luke's for eighteen months following the ending of a difficult placement with another family. Mr and Mrs C. were in their late 30s, had been married three years and had not been able to have a child of their own.

Mr and Mrs C. had been approved as adoptive parents and they recalled the home study and the waiting for the panel decision as a disturbing experience. Ultimately it was agreed that a possible placement of Martin should be explored further.

Mrs C.   Our social worker told us that the next step was for John to visit us. We understood it was because he knew Martin well, to see whether he would fit in with us. I cannot remember everything that was said, but we had confidence in John.

Mr C.   I think we felt, we like this chap, he knows what he is doing.

Mrs C.   Having heard more from John about Martin we were very keen to meet him. However, when John described how the meetings would happen, how everything was child orientated, I thought 'the man's crazy'. Over a period of a few weeks, I began to realize how sensible the programme was and began to see Martin blossoming and looking forward to see us.

124

John discussed Mr and Mrs C. with the other members of the team, a case conference was held and agreement was reached to go ahead with introductions. The first visit to St Luke's for Mr and Mrs C. was arranged. The plan was for Martin to meet them, but he was not to be told the purpose of the visit. This meeting is described in chapter 7 from our viewpoint. How did Martin, now 16, remember that visit?

Martin   It was in the conference room; I thought I had been tricked, because I had to do some recorder practice. I was told to do it in the conference room, but I'd never done it there before, so I thought something must be on. I thought it was a sneaky way to do introductions, but if I had been told, that would have been scary. It really was a good way to do it.

Mr and Mrs C. also have a vivid memory of that first meeting:

Mr C.   Our car broke down on the way and we had to get a train to London and it produced a response in us that we had not realized was there. We didn't realize how much we were keyed up but this brought our feelings to the surface.

Mrs C.   I remember Brenda saying on the phone, when the car broke down: 'Do you think it's worth trying to come on to London?' and suggesting we postpone our visit. I remember saying to Terry: 'If we don't go today, I don't want to know.' I felt it was so important to get there to make that initial contact. The first thing I remember of St Luke's was being in the conference room. A few minutes later in came Martin, very shy, and would not face us. He was supposed to be having a recorder lesson. I think he was persuaded to address a few words to us, but not very many and they were about dinosaurs. The recorder lesson didn't go very well.

Mr C.   I just remember this very shy figure lurking, who wanted to take peeps up, but only for a fleeting moment.

Mrs C.   Even if the process did not fool Martin, the pretence was probably a good thing. For a more forthright child, a straightforward introduction might have been more appropriate. For Martin, he could have a look at us without any sense of commitment or challenge.

How did they feel at the end of the visit?

Mr C.   I remeber chuckling at this very shy little figure.

Mrs C.   I can remember very vividly the tube journey back to Paddington and feeling turned over and thinking, what have we achieved? It seemed so pointless – all that anticipation, that journey, and we had not got very far. I thought Martin would never be able to say he wanted to come and live with us.

Over the next seven weeks, Mr and Mrs C. were to make fourteen visits to St Luke's. How did they and Martin perceive what was happening?

Martin   After that visit they came to see me several times. I was interested in prehistoric monsters. I had been given a book about them. We went to see some stone ones at Crystal Palace Park and also went to the Science Museum. I did not think of Jean and Terry as future parents, but more as someone to take me out.

Mrs C.   I remember John saying, the first time we took Martin out, that he would want to take something from St Luke's with him and I thought what on earth for, but he did. He took some Lego and it had to be in his pocket. As we got to know Martin, he seemed so right for us.

Mr C.   I remember some sense of frustration. We were intent on building a relationship which didn't have time for a relapse, which is why we wanted the visits to St Luke's to be closer together. We didn't feel conscious of tiredness, but a need to get on with it.

At the end of each visit a discussion took place between Bill or Brenda and Mr and Mrs C. about the events of the day.

Mrs C.   These discussions were very helpful, assessing where we were at and sorting out the next step.

Mr C.   We were impressed with the relationships the staff

had with all the children at St Luke's and the way we
were drawn into the relationship with Martin and
the way each step was explained, or the significance
of a specific incident.

Mrs C.   All the way through, the discussions were about the
way Martin would react at each stage, and he did.
This was the thing that absolutely floored me – he
did do all the things the staff said he would do. I was
fascinated.

Eventually the time arrived for Martin to visit the home of
Mr and Mrs C.; day visits at first, then an overnight stay and
gradually building up to placement. Throughout the introduction process, Martin found direct communication with the
Unit's staff difficult and the reader will recall from chapter 7
that he involved another child and his special house-mother to
relay his feeling about contact with Mr and Mrs C. Martin
remembers a little of those visits to Mr and Mrs C.'s home, and
spoke of how he views the process now.

Martin   I remember visiting the school, also having chicken-
pox, which meant I did not have to go back to St
Luke's for a while. I liked that. The time it took to
visit was good because it built up the relationship so
that when I left St Luke's I felt it was very strong. I
don't remember any discussions, but I think I asked
to go to live with my new family.

Mr C.   It was during these visits that the one point arose
where we queried John's judgement, and that was
over the way Martin was brought into something
for his reaction to issues. We felt it was too formal
and artificial, with Martin needing to behave in a
special way rather than relaxing and being himself.
When faced with a question, it was as though he was
on the edge of his seat and his answer was always
'that's a very difficult question'.

Looking back, we recognize that our own anxieties were
showing because we were having difficulty in communicating
with Martin. We tried too hard, causing us to be over-cautious
and unable to realize that his attachments were with his new
family, to whom he was communicating his feelings.

Mrs C.   Martin came for nearly a week at half-term and he
was to go back on the Friday, and when we waved
him off I was really upset. He was going back to
school for a short time and I felt this was regressive.
I can remember he came the following weekend. A
lot of the St Luke's children had chicken-pox.
Martin found his spots as soon as he got here, and
he was absolutely miserable until the doctor
pronounced chicken-pox and then his face beamed
as if to say: 'they can't send me back'. It was really
very funny and I think we felt that St Luke's would
agree with that.

The staff of St Luke's did share the joke. Three days before, we
had realized that, if Martin was going to get chicken-pox, it was
likely to happen around the time of his visit to Mr and Mrs C.
and that, if the spots had appeared before he left St Luke's, the
visit would have had to be postponed. Consequently, the Unit's
staff, feeling that we had reached a critical stage of the process,
agreed that as long as no other symptoms appeared we would
not look too hard for the tell-tale spots.

By this time we had a clearer understanding of how Martin
was feeling. We had looked back at the case record, to see if we
had missed clues about how Martin was feeling about Mr and
Mrs C. We found plenty of indirect references which,
somehow, we had missed. For example, after his first visit to
the home of Mr and Mrs C., he had referred to the family's dog
as 'our dog' and their car as 'our car'. On the morning of the
second visit, when his special house-mother went to wake him,
she found him lying in bed fully dressed. For a subsequent visit,
it had been suggested that John escort Martin only halfway, the
remainder of the journey being made with the family's social
worker. When this suggestion was put to Martin, he replied: 'I
don't care.' When asked to explain what he meant he replied: 'I
don't care who takes me to —'. After his next visit, he actually
said: 'I would like to live with Mr and Mrs C.', but then added a
number of reservations. This was, in fact, his normal pattern of
behaviour and 'but if' regularly punctuated his conversation.
Instead of accepting that Martin always qualified important
statements, we became cautious because of his qualifying

comments. Putting all the pieces of information together made us realize that we were in danger of missing the opportune moment to move Martin. We had already missed a number of clues and, if Martin had missed out on his next visit because of chicken-pox, we could envisage the placement being put at risk.

However, after this visit John recorded:

Although fairly relaxed when it came to making sure he had his belongings packed, Martin really did not want to know and embarked on a series of diversionary tactics, culminating in doing his best to prevent me from opening the car door. Eventually, he got into the car, but commented: 'I hope your engine blows up before it starts.' Discussion of why he wanted this to happen just produced evasiveness. For most of the journey he was fairly relaxed, although any reference to Mr and Mrs C. or the town they lived in only had the effect of making him 'grumble'. At one point he said somewhat disconsolately: 'I am fed up with travelling.' I asked him whether, in that case, he wanted to stay at St Luke's, at which he became very angry and said: 'I don't mean that.' I asked him what he did mean and he replied: 'When I get back to St Luke's, I want to go back to Mr and Mrs C. and stay. I don't want to live at St Luke's.'

It was then definitely decided that Martin should go to live with Mr and Mrs C., a day he was later to describe as 'my happiest day'.

Martin	When I arrived everything went pretty quickly, and starting a new school, once I settled down, helped.
Mr C.	It was good to have Martin here and more settled, but the problems we had heard about, where were they?
Mrs C.	Martin's basic personality, the sulks and depressions Bill, Brenda and John had told us about were there, but if we were patient they passed. Subsequently, we realised how important it was that Martin was our first child.
Mr C.	He needed time with a new family for himself.

Martin, like other children, took his past with him into placement and needed to share it with his new family, as well as to compare it with this new experience.

Mrs C.   He talked a little about St Luke's, in particular one child with whom he had had an important relationship. He talked a lot about his previous foster family and still does, particularly the problems and the hates.

In the time that followed the family's social worker had the responsibility for the statutory supervision of the placement and was a welcome visitor, although Martin was, as ever, down to earth on the subject.

Martin   I remember him visiting. I thought he was quite nice because he gave me a tractor for Christmas.

Mr C.   It was very comforting to have his support and to know that help was available if we needed it.

For a short while John also visited Martin. Was this an inconvenience for the family?

Mr C.   I was warmed by it; that Martin wasn't simply being written off, severed from his past, but he was being allowed some continuity and trouble was being taken over this. Martin had bad feelings about some of his past, but it was good that he was allowed to keep a connection with a bit of his past that he had good feelings about.

Mrs C.   Martin thought John was quite special.

In June 1978 Mr and Mrs C. were granted an adoption order. How significant was this to Martin and his family?

Martin   I was told a lot about adoption and it was important to me. I thought it would take a long time in Court, but it was all over very quickly.

Mr C.   The adoption hearing was significant for Martin; he realised the commitment involved.

Mrs C.   Coming up to the point of the adoption hearing, he still had not got over the tendency of not giving straight answers. We explained the judge would ask him straight questions and would want straight answers. In fact no questions were asked and Martin was furious!

Since then three other children have been placed with Mr and Mrs C. The length and methods of introduction were very different, because they were different children with different needs. We believe it is important to approach each new placement as a new piece of work, which will need to be tailored to the needs of the individuals involved rather than follow set patterns which are geared to making the professionals comfortable.

CONCLUSIONS

The children in the Long-Stay Unit at St Luke's, like so many children in public care, had long histories of failed bonding or attachment to their own families and, in many cases, they had had the same experiences in a number of substitute families. In working with them, we had to recognize that they brought with them their very distinctive life experiences. Consequently with each child we had to focus on his individual experiences and needs, in order to plan for his future.

Children whose close relationships have been predominantly negative need to learn how to make positive attachments, irrespective of whether the plan is for them to return to their birth family or to be placed with a new family. Unless children are helped to learn in this area, their negative experiences will ensure that they will continue to fail to make attachments, with the result that potentially good plans end in failure.[1] However, attachments formed at St Luke's formed a bridge into the future.

Many of the children who were placed in new families from St Luke's are now either adults or well into adolescence. Some of their families, as with any other group of families, have had their share of pain and distress dealt them by the unpredictability of life. We are grateful that, in spite of these hazards, the children we were privileged to work with have not only retained but developed the positive, enriching relationships with their new families which they had so much needed. It would seem fitting, therefore, to end this book with the words of one of those children, Martin, now a young man, who said of his placement: 'It's wonderful, it's home.'

Notes

INTRODUCTION: THE NEED FOR PERMANENCE

1 Jane Rowe and Lydia Lambert, *Children Who Wait*, Association of British Adoption Agencies, 1973, p.39.
2 Bill Jordan, 'Prevention', *Adoption and Fostering*, 105 (3), 1981, p. 21.
3 Christine Cooper, 'Paediatric Aspects', in M. Adcock and R. White (eds.), *Terminating Parental Contact: An Exploration of the Issues relating to Children in Care,* British Agencies for Adoption and Fostering, 1980, p. 35.
4 R. A. Parker, *Planning for Deprived Children*, National Children's Home, 1971, p. 50.
5 E. Cole, 'Conflicting Rights', *Adoption and Fostering*, 95 (1), 1979, p. 36.
6 Ibid.

2 OUR PHILOSOPHY AND APPROACH

1 O. Stevenson, 'Reception into Care: its meaning for all concerned', *Case Conference*, 10 (4), September 1963, p. 110.

3 COMMUNICATING WITH CHILDREN

1 Guisela Kanopka, *The Adolescent Girl in Conflict*, Prentice Hall, 1966, p. 16.

6 PLANNING FOR FAMILY PLACEMENT

1 N. Kay, 'A Systematic Approach to Selecting Foster Parents', *Case Conference*, 13 (2), June 1966, p. 45.

10 REFLECTIONS

1 V. Fahlberg, *Attachment and Separation*, British Agencies for Adoption and Fostering, 1981, pp. 1–8.

Further Reading

K. Donley, *Opening New Doors,* Association of British Adoption Agencies, 1975

For Ever and Ever, Association of British Adoption Agencies, 1975

Dorothy M. Jeffree, Roy McConkey and Simon Hewson, *Let Me Play*, Souvenir Press, 1977

Barbara Tizard, *Adoption: A Second Chance*, Open Books, 1977

D. W. Winnicott, *The Family and Individual Development*, Social Science Paperbacks in association with Tavistock Publications, 1965

Sula Wolff, *Children Under Stress*, Allen Lane/Penguin Books, 1969

Working Together – A Guide to the Policy, Procedure and Practice of Inter-Agency Adoption Placements, Adoption Resource Exchange, 1980

Working with Children who are Joining New Families, Association of British Adoption and Fostering Agencies, 1977

Index